Learn Docker
Java, Node.JS, PHP or Python

Be ready to create and run your containerized application next week.

Arnaud Weil

Learn Docker - .NET Core, Java, Node.JS, PHP or Python

Be ready to create and run your containerized application next week.

Arnaud Weil

ISBN 978-0-244-76522-4

© 2018 - 2019 Arnaud Weil

To Christophe Gouguenheim, for getting me to write my first book a few years ago.

To my parents, for teaching me freedom and making sure I can enjoy it.

To my wonderful family. Your love and support fueled this book.

To my readers who suggested improvements to this book, especially Doğan Kartaltepe for your ongoing and dedicated support.

Contents

Introduction i
    What this book is not i
    Prerequisites i
    How to read this book ii
    Tools you need ii
    Source code iii

1. Why Docker? **1**
    1.1 A DevOps enabler tool 1
    1.2 It solves dependency conflicts 3
    1.3 It allows for easy scaling up 5
    1.4 It allows for seamless upgrades 7
    1.5 International commerce already uses containers 9

2. Get Docker up and running **13**
    2.1 Various products for various needs 13
    2.2 Community on a developer or CI machine 14
    2.3 Enterprise on a Server 16

3. Basic concepts **19**

CONTENTS

4. Use Docker images **21**
    4.1   Do-it-yourself: run a container 21
    4.2   Container management commands 23
    4.3   Do-it-yourself: post-mortem inspection . 24
    4.4   More about docker run 26
    4.5   Running a server container 29
    4.6   Exercise - Run a server container 40
    4.7   Exercise solution 40
    4.8   Using volumes 42
    4.9   Where do images come from? 43

5. Create Docker images **47**
    5.1   Creating a simple image 47
    5.2   Creating an image including files 51
    5.3   Images are created locally 54
    5.4   Exercise - Build an image and run it . . . 56
    5.5   Exercise solution 57
    5.6   Tags matter 58
    5.7   Parameters as environment variables . . . 62
    5.8   Exercise - Enable an image to be parameterized 67
    5.9   Exercise solution 68
    5.10 Storage 70
    5.11 Networking 71
    5.12 Learning more 71

6. Publish Docker images **73**
    6.1   Rationale for publishing 73
    6.2   Registries 75
    6.3   Publishing an image 75
    6.4   Docker Hub 76

	6.5	Run an image on another machine	79
	6.6	Exercise - Publish an image and run a container on another machine	81
	6.7	Exercise solution	81
	6.8	Private registries	83
	6.9	Size matters	84
7.	**Forget SDK installs**		**97**
	7.1	One tool to rule them all	97
	7.2	Building rationally: easy CI	98
	7.3	Multi-stage dockerfiles	100
8.	**Docker with common development profiles**		**105**
	8.1	.NET Core	105
	8.2	Java	112
	8.3	Node.JS	113
	8.4	PHP	117
	8.5	Python	119
9.	**More about Running containers**		**123**
	9.1	Restart mode	123
	9.2	Monitoring	124
	9.3	Reclaim your disk	125
	9.4	Orchestration basics	126

Image attributions **131**

A word from the author **133**

The Learn collection **135**

Introduction

What this book is not

I made my best to keep this book small, so that you can learn Docker quickly without getting lost in petty details. If you are looking for a reference book where you'll find answers to all the questions you may have within the next 4 years of your Docker practice, you'll find other heavy books for that.

My purpose is to swiftly provide you with the tools you need to create and run your first containerized application using Docker, then be able to look for more by yourself when needed. While some authors seem to pride themselves in having the thickest book, in this series I'm glad I achieved the thinnest possible book for my purpose. Though I tried my best to keep all of what seems necessary, based on my 16 years experience of teaching.

Prerequisites

In order for this book to meet its goals, you must have basic experience creating applications with **one** of the following technologies: .NET Core, Java, Node.JS, PHP or Python.

How to read this book

This book's aim is to make you productive as quickly as possible. For this we'll use some theory, several demonstrations, plus exercises. Exercises appear like the following:

> Do it yourself: Time to grab your keyboard and code away to meet the given objectives.

In code samples, a backslash is used in order to wrap long lines. Do not type theses backslashes when you copy code from the book.

Tools you need

The only tools you'll need to work through this book are the following:

- A Windows, Linux or Mac machine that meets the specifications for Docker Engine or Docker Desktop.
- A GIT client.
- A text editor.

Source code

All of the source code for the demos and do-it-yourself solutions is available at https://bitbucket.org/epobb/dockerbookfiles

It can be downloaded as a ZIP file[1], or if you installed GIT you can simply type:

```
git clone https://bitbucket.org/epobb/dockerbookfiles.g\
it
```

---
[1] https://bitbucket.org/epobb/dockerbookfiles/downloads

1. Why Docker?

If you're in a hurry, you can safely skip this chapter and head straight to the Get Docker up and running chapter. This *Why Docker?* chapter is there for those that want to know why containers should be used.

1.1 A DevOps enabler tool

Docker is an engine that runs containers, and containers as a tool allow to solve many challenges created by the growing DevOps trend.

In DevOps, the Dev and Ops teams have conflicting goals:

Dev team seeks	Ops team seeks
Frequent deployments and updates	Stability of production apps
Easy creation of new resources	Manage infrastructure, not applications
	Monitoring and control

As an agile developer I want to frequently publish my applications so that deployment becomes a routine. The rationale behind this is that this agility makes the "go to production" event a normal, frequent, completely mastered event instead of a dreaded disaster that may awake monsters who will hit me one week later. On the other hand, it is the Ops team that will have to face the user if anything goes wrong in deployment - so they naturally want stability.

Containers ease deployment because deploying is as simple as running a new container, routing users to the new one, and trashing the old one. It can even be automated by orchestration tools, and since it's dead easy we can afford to have many containers serving a single application for increased stability during updates.

If you don't use containers, Ops need to handle your hosting environment: runtimes, libraries, OS needed by your application. On the other side, when using containers they just need one single methodology that can handle the containers you provide no matter what's inside them. You may as well use .NET Core, Java, Node.JS, PHP, Python or another development tool: it doesn't matter to them as long as your code is containerized. This is a huge advantage for containers when it comes to DevOps.

In the Docker with common development profiles chapter we'll see how to create container images for specific development technologies. But your Ops don't see how you create the images, they just see container images.

1.2 It solves dependency conflicts

A typical web application looks something like the following:

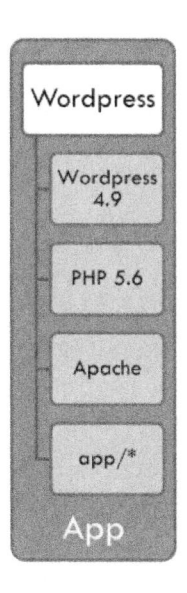

The application is made of files served by an HTTP server (Apache here, but it could be Kestrel, IIS, NGINX, ...), a runtime (PHP 5.6 here) and a development framework (Wordpress 4.9 here).

Without containers, the dependencies and files are all placed together on a server. Since managing those dependencies is time-consuming, similar apps are typically grouped on the same server, sharing their dependencies:

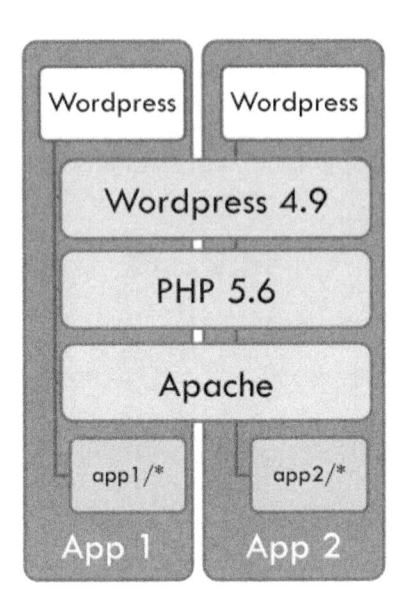

Now suppose you want to upgrade the PHP runtime from version 5.6 to 7.2. But the version change induces breaking changes in the applications that hence need to be updated. You need to update both *App 1* and *App 2* when proceeding with the upgrade. On a server that may host many apps of this type, this is going to be a daunting task and you'll need to delay the upgrade until all apps are ready.

Another similar problem is when you want to host say *App 3* on the same server, but *App 3* uses the Node.JS runtime together with a package that when installed changes a dependency that is used by the PHP runtime. Conflicts between runtimes are not scarce, so you probably faced that problem already.

Containers solve this problem because each app is going to run inside its own container with its own dependencies. Your typical server would look like:

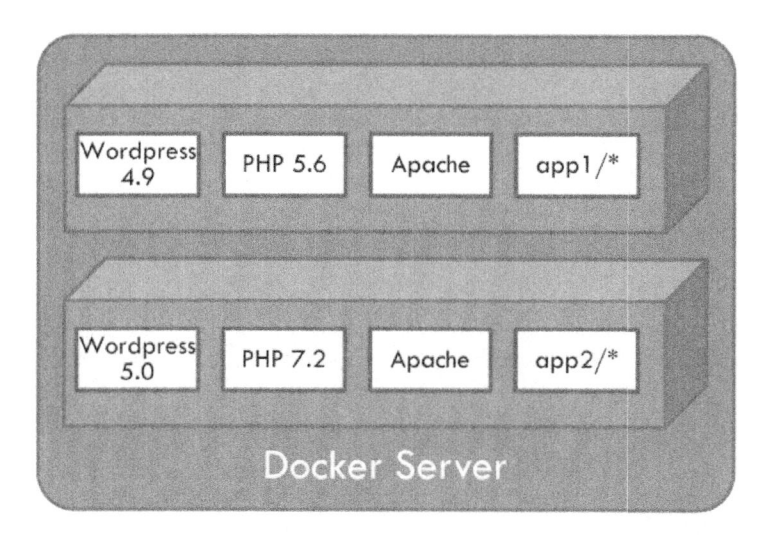

```
┌─────────────────────────────────────────────┐
│  Wordpress   PHP 5.6   Apache    app1/*     │
│     4.9                                     │
├─────────────────────────────────────────────┤
│  Wordpress   PHP 7.2   Apache    app2/*     │
│     5.0                                     │
│              Docker Server                  │
└─────────────────────────────────────────────┘
```

Each container encapsulates its own dependencies. Which means you can migrate the PHP runtime from version 5.6 to 7.2 in a container without affecting other. Any other container that would use, e.g., Node.JS would not interfere with any of the Wordpress containers.

1.3 It allows for easy scaling up

When a server application needs to handle a higher usage than what a single server can handle, the solution is well-known: place a reverse proxy in front of it, and duplicate the server as many times as needed. In our previous Wordpress application example, this means duplicating the server together with all of its dependencies:

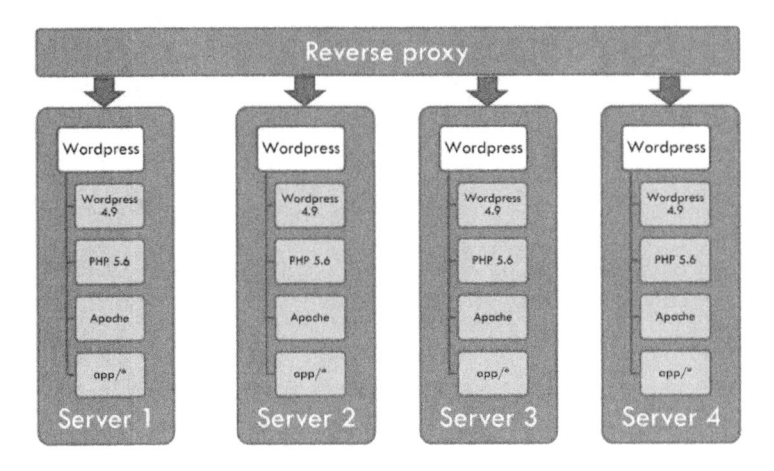

[Figure: Reverse proxy distributing to Server 1, Server 2, Server 3, Server 4 — each containing Wordpress, Wordpress 4.9, PHP 5.6, Apache, app/*]

That is only going to make things worse when upgrading: we'll need to upgrade each server's dependencies, together with all of the conflicts that may induce.

Again, containers have a solution for this. As we'll see in the Basic concepts section, containers are based on images. You simply need to run as many containers as you wish from a single image, and they will all sport the exact same dependencies.

Better yet: when using an orchestrator you simply need to state how many containers you want, the image name, and the orchestrator will create that many containers on all of your Docker servers. We'll see this in the orchestrators part. This is how it looks:

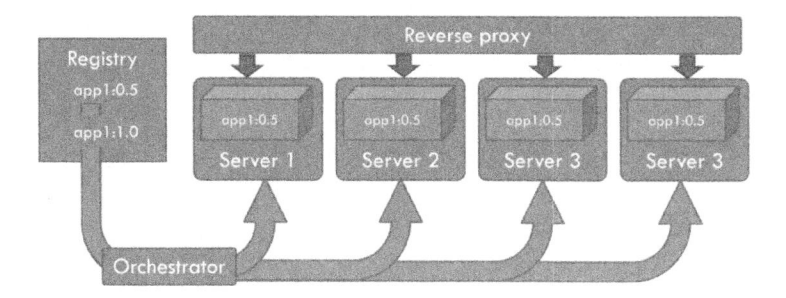

1.4 It allows for seamless upgrades

Even in scaled-up scenarios, a container-based approach makes trivial a concept that would otherwise be tricky. Without containers, your favorite admin will not be happy with you if he has to update every server including the dependencies:

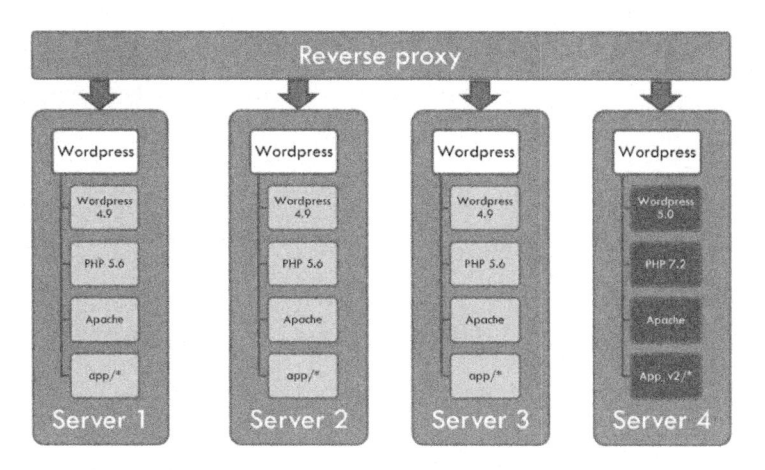

Of course, in such a case the update process will depend on the application and its dependencies. Don't even try to tell your admins about DevOps if you want to remain alive.

By using containers, it's a simple matter of telling the orchestrator that you want to run a new image version, and it will gradually replace every container with another one running the new version. Whatever the technology stack running inside the containers, it's a simple command (in fact, by changing just one line as we'll see).

The illustration below shows the process as it goes on: the orchestrator replaces one container, and will then move on to the other ones. While the new container is not ready, traffic is being routed to the old version containers so that there is no interruption of service.

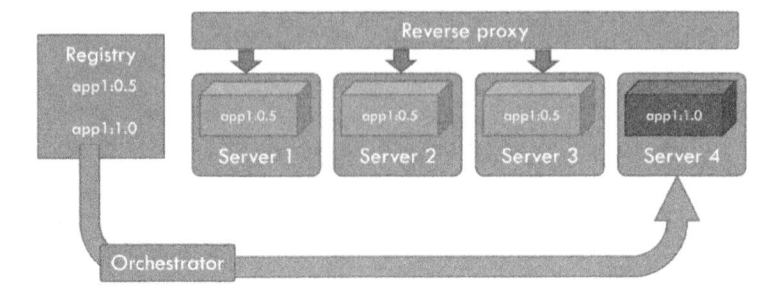

1.5 International commerce already uses containers

Sure, you may wonder why I make such a comparison. You may even be trying to evaluate how crazy I am or wondering whether to return this book where you bought it. Wonder no more: I'm not crazy. International commerce faced the same delivery problem: we are trying to deliver software as fluently as possible, and commerce needs to deliver goods as fluently as possible.

In the old times, it took days to load a ship with goods:

Classic ship loading

The ship remained docked at the pier during a few days while each good was being loaded into it. Goods had varying sizes and handling precautions, and ships had storage of varying types and sizes. That's what made loading (and unloading) a slow process. Slow and costly: it required many people to do it, plus the immobilization of the ship and goods has a cost.

A solution was found: containers. The idea is very simple: use boxes of a standard size, and fill them with whatever you want. You now only need to handle standardized boxes no matter what they contain. Problem solved: the ship can be tailored to host many containers in a way that allow for fast (un)loading thanks to standardized tools like cranes:

Container ship loading

In fact, the whole transport chain (trains, trucks) can be tailored to manage containers efficiently:

Freight train

Believe it or not: Docker containers are very similar. When you create an image, you stuff your software into a container image. When a machine runs it, a container is created from the image. Container images and containers can be managed in a standardized way, which allows for standard solutions during a containerized software's lifecycle:

- common build chain;
- common image storage;
- common way to deploy and scale up;
- common hosting of running containers;
- common control and monitoring of running containers;
- common ways to update running containers to a new version.

The most important part being: whatever the real software inside the container, it can be handled in a common way. Isn't that a DevOps' dream?

2. Get Docker up and running

2.1 Various products for various needs

In a production environment that runs containers that host critical applications, you'd rather let your favorite admins install *Docker Enterprise*.

On your development machine or a continuous integration build machine though, you can simply use the free *Docker Engine Community* or *Docker Desktop* (depending on your machine type).

In short:

Use	Product
Developer machine	*Docker Engine Community* or *Docker Desktop*
Small server, small expectations	*Docker Engine Community*
Serious stuff	*Docker Engine Enterprise* or *Kubernetes*

The rest of this chapter will point you to installation steps for various platforms.

Hello world test

Whatever the edition you install, you can check your installation by running the following command in a command-line (your terminal on Linux, or PowerShell on Windows):

```
docker run hello-world
```

It should pull an image and output text that begins with:

```
Hello from Docker!
This message shows that your installation appears to be\
 working correctly.
```

2.2 Community on a developer or CI machine

Windows 10

Docker Desktop requires a Professional or Enterprise 64-bit edition of Windows 10, because it is based on Hyper-V.

> In case you have a desktop version of Windows that doesn't meet the requirements, you may use the older Docker Toolbox[a] based on VirtualBox.
>
> [a]https://docs.docker.com/toolbox/overview/

Before you install Docker Desktop it's important that you:

- enable Hyper-V
- enable hardware virtualization in the BIOS

Then, follow this link[1] and follow the instructions found there.

Linux

There are other Docker packages available and you can simply follow the steps depending on your version:

- CentOS 7[2]
- Debian or Raspbian[3]
- Fedora 26+ 64-bit[4]
- Ubuntu Bionic, Xenial or Trusty 64-bit[5]

---

[1]https://docs.docker.com/docker-for-windows/install/
[2]https://docs.docker.com/install/linux/docker-ce/centos/
[3]https://docs.docker.com/engine/installation/linux/debian/
[4]https://docs.docker.com/engine/installation/linux/fedora/
[5]https://docs.docker.com/install/linux/docker-ce/ubuntu/

Whatever your Linux flavor, there are common post-installation steps here[6]. Make sure that you read them carefully, more so if you cannot successfully run the hello-world test.

Mac

Docker Desktop requires a Mac OS Sierra 10.12 or above.

> In case you have an older macOS version, you may use the older Docker Toolbox[a] based on VirtualBox.
> [a]https://docs.docker.com/toolbox/overview/

At the bottom of this page[7] are the instructions on installing *Docker Desktop*.

2.3 Enterprise on a Server

Windows Server 2016

Docker Enterprise is available at no additional cost to Windows Server 2016 customers. Just follow the instructions[8].

---
[6]https://docs.docker.com/install/linux/linux-postinstall/
[7]https://hub.docker.com/editions/community/docker-ce-desktop-mac
[8]https://docs.docker.com/install/windows/docker-ee/#system-requirements

Linux

Docker Enterprise can be ran on CentOs, Red Hat, SUSE, Ubuntu and more. Check here[9] to see if your edition of Linux is supported.

Cloud

Docker Enterprise is available as a template for Azure[10] and for AWS[11].

---
[9] https://hub.docker.com/search/?type=edition&offering=enterprise
[10] https://hub.docker.com/editions/enterprise/docker-ee-azure
[11] https://hub.docker.com/editions/enterprise/docker-ee-aws

3. Basic concepts

There are three concepts I need you to grasp so that we can begin smoothly: **containers**, **images** and **registries**.

A *container* is what we eventually want to run and host in Docker. You can think of it as an isolated machine. Or a virtual machine if you prefer.

From a conceptual point of view, a *container* runs inside the Docker host isolated from the other containers and even the host OS. It cannot see the other containers, physical storage, or get incoming connections unless you explicitly state that it can. It contains everything it needs to run: OS, packages, runtimes, files, environment variables, standard input and output.

Your typical Docker server would look like this - a host for many containers:

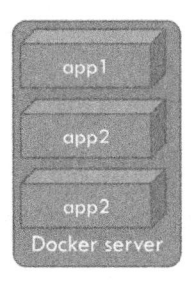

The fact that there are two *app2* containers in the schema above is normal: this is typically the case when a server hosts a release and a test version. Which means you could host both versions on the same server. In fact, each container has its own ID but let's keep things simple for now.

Any container that runs is created from an *image*. An image describes everything that is needed to create a container: it is a template for containers. You may create as many containers as needed from a single image.

The whole picture looks like:

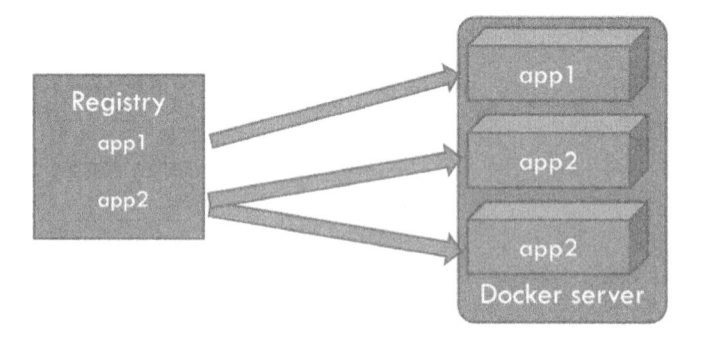

Images are stored in a *registry*. In the example above, the *app2* image is used to create two containers. Each container lives its own life, and they both share a common root: their image from the registry.

In the next chapters, you're going to learn how to run containers from existing images, then you'll learn to create your own images and upload them to registries.

4. Use Docker images

4.1 Do-it-yourself: run a container

Run the following command on a command-line:

```
docker run hello-world
```

You can see the following text output:

```
Windows PowerShell
PS C:\> docker run hello-world
Unable to find image 'hello-world:latest' locally
latest: Pulling from library/hello-world
d1725b59e92d: Pull complete
Digest: sha256:b3a26e22bf55e4a5232b391281fc1673f18462b75cdc76aa103e6d3a2bce5e77
Status: Downloaded newer image for hello-world:latest

Hello from Docker!
This message shows that your installation appears to be working correctly.

To generate this message, Docker took the following steps:
 1. The Docker client contacted the Docker daemon.
 2. The Docker daemon pulled the "hello-world" image from the Docker Hub.
    (amd64)
 3. The Docker daemon created a new container from that image which runs the
    executable that produces the output you are currently reading.
 4. The Docker daemon streamed that output to the Docker client, which sent it
    to your terminal.

To try something more ambitious, you can run an Ubuntu container with:
 $ docker run -it ubuntu bash

Share images, automate workflows, and more with a free Docker ID:
 https://hub.docker.com/

For more examples and ideas, visit:
 https://docs.docker.com/get-started/

PS C:\>
```

Congratulations, you just ran your first container! Here's what just happened in detail:

1. Your command asks Docker to create and run a container based on the *hello-world* image.
2. Since the *hello-world* image wasn't present already on your disk, Docker downloaded it from a default registry, the *Docker Hub*. More about that later.
3. Docker created a container based on the *hello-world* image.
4. The *hello-world* image states that when started it should output some text to the console, so this is the text you see as the container is ran.
5. The container stopped.

Here's what you did, slightly simplified:

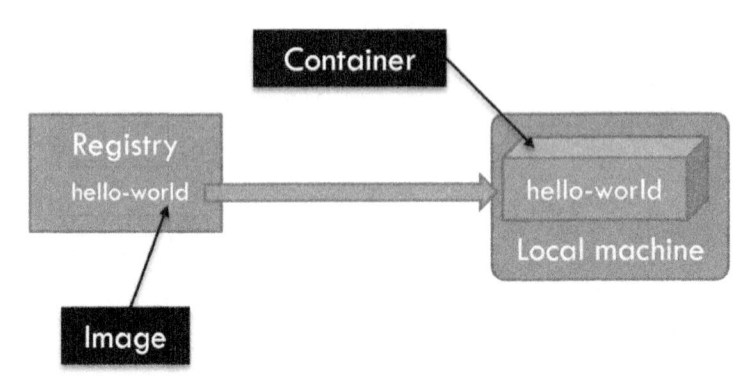

If you run exactly the same command again, you'll see that all steps above are repeated except for step 2: since the image is already present on your machine, it is not downloaded again. This is a simple optimization, but you'll see later that Docker optimizes many more steps. As such, Docker makes scarce use of a machine's resources.

4.2 Container management commands

You can get help for Docker commands from the command-line itself using the *–help* switch. For instance, in order to know more about the *docker run* command we just used, you could type:

```
docker run --help
```

You may use the following commands for container management:

- docker ps: lists the containers that are still running. Add the **-a** switch in order to see containers that stopped.
- docker logs: retrieves the logs of a container, even when it has stopped.
- docker inspect: get detailed information about a running or stopped container.
- docker stop: delete a container that is still running.
- docker rm: delete a container.

4.3 Do-it-yourself: post-mortem inspection

The container we ran previously stopped because its only job was to output some text. We'll soon run more advanced containers, but let's play with that stopped container in order to get to grips with the container tooling.

Run the following command on a command-line:

```
docker ps
```

There is no output because no container is currently running on your machine. Now run the following command on a command-line:

```
docker ps -a
```

You should see output similar to the one below (the exact container ID varies):

Container ID	Image	Status
48bab7f673b3	hello-world	Exited

Note the container ID. It allows you to run commands on that container.

Run the following command (replacing the ID with your container ID):

```
docker logs 48bab7f673b3
```

That command outputs exactly the same text you saw when you ran the container. This is the standard output of the container. In real-world scenarios, you'll have containers running in the background (web servers for instance) and that command will allow you to have a look at their output.

Run the following command (replacing the ID with your container ID):

```
docker inspect 48bab7f673b3
```

That gets you lots of information about many aspects of the container - whether it is still running or stopped. Again, in real-world scenarios that may prove useful for understanding what happens to inside your containers.

All of that information takes up space and once you're completely done with a stopped container you may want to reclaim that space. That's what the *docker rm* command is for.

Run the following command (replacing the ID with your container ID):

```
docker rm 48bab7f673b3
```

Now you can make sure that the container isn't there anymore by running the above commands:

```
docker ps -a
docker logs 48bab7f673b3
docker inspect 48bab7f673b3
```

Docker doesn't know about that container anymore:

```
PS C:\> docker ps -a
CONTAINER ID    IMAGE           COMMAND         CREATED         S
TATUS           PORTS           NAMES
PS C:\> docker logs 48bab7f673b3
Error: No such container: 48bab7f673b3
PS C:\> docker inspect 48bab7f673b3
[]
Error: No such object: 48bab7f673b3
PS C:\>
```

4.4 More about docker run

You can think of the *docker run* command as the equivalent of buying a new computer, executing some command on it, then trashing it. Really. Each time a container is created from an image you get a new isolated and virgin environment to play with inside the container.

What you get inside the container depends on which image your container is based on. After the image name, you can pass commands to execute inside the container.

Let's illustrate the new-computer-that-you-trash metaphor using the *alpine* image. The *alpine* image is a very small Linux image that does enough for our purpose.

Let's run a container and ask it to display its hostname.

```
docker run alpine printenv
```

We basically ask for a container to be created using the *alpine* image, and for the container to execute the *printenv* command that is one of the binary programs packed in the *alpine* image.

Without surprise, the *alpine* image is downloaded in order to create the container, since it was not present on my disk already.

The result is the following:

```
PS C:\> docker run alpine printenv
Unable to find image 'alpine:latest' locally
latest: Pulling from library/alpine
cd784148e348: Pull complete
Digest: sha256:46e71df1e5191ab8b8034c5189e325258ec44ea739bba1e5645cff83
c9048ff1
Status: Downloaded newer image for alpine:latest
PATH=/usr/local/sbin:/usr/local/bin:/usr/sbin:/usr/bin:/sbin:/bin
HOSTNAME=b4fe06a89b62
HOME=/root
PS C:\>
```

Now let's run two more containers and ask them to display their respective hostnames.

```
docker run alpine printenv
docker run alpine printenv
```

This is the same command as above, repeated twice. On each line we're asking for a new container to be created using the *alpine* image, and for the container to execute the *printenv* command.

The *alpine* image isn't downloaded because it is already on our disk. Two more independent containers are created. The result is the following:

```
PS C:\> docker run alpine printenv
PATH=/usr/local/sbin:/usr/local/bin:/usr/sbin:/usr/bin:/sbin:/bin
HOSTNAME=7eadf520db74
HOME=/root
PS C:\> docker run alpine printenv
PATH=/usr/local/sbin:/usr/local/bin:/usr/sbin:/usr/bin:/sbin:/bin
HOSTNAME=7ca6722e214e
HOME=/root
PS C:\>
```

Note that inside each container the displayed *hostname* is different. See? You get the equivalent of a new machine on each container.

Here is a simplified schema of what I did:

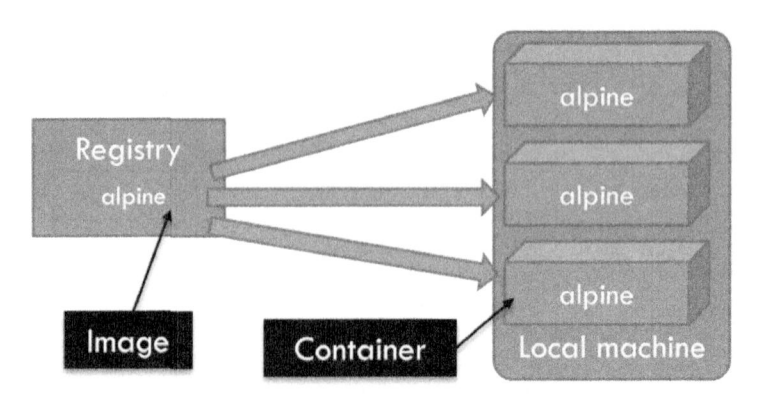

What I want you to understand is that Docker is a tool that allows you to get the equivalent of a disposable, single-time use computer. Once you get that clear, a whole new world opens for you. You come from a world where obtaining a new machine and configuring it required enough efforts to justify keeping it, with all the side effects that meant on each subsequent use; in the containers' world, getting a brand new environment is cheap enough for us to get many, many of them.

If I list the stopped containers on my machine (docker ps -a) I'll get 3 stopped containers since I just asked for that number of containers to be created. Being quite lazy, I don't want to remove them one by one, so I use the following handy command:

```
docker container prune -f
```

This is simply the equivalent of running one *docker rm* command for each stopped container. The *-f* switch is an implicit confirmation to proceed and delete all stopped containers right away, instead of asking to confirm that operation.

4.5 Running a server container

We just saw how to run short-lived containers. They usually do some processing and output something. There's a very common use for long-lived containers however: server containers. Whether you want to host a web application, an API or a database, you want a container that listens for incoming network connections and is potentially long-lived.

> A word of warning: it's best not to think about containers as long-lived, even when they are. Don't store information inside the containers. In other words, ensure your containers are stateless not stateful. We'll see later how and where to store your container's state. Docker containers are very stable, but the reason for having stateless containers is that this allows for easy scaling up and recovery. More about that later.

In short, a server container

- is long-lived;
- listens for incoming network connections.

How can we manage that ? Read on.

Running a long-lived container

Up to now we remained connected to the container from our command line using the *docker run* command. That makes it impractical for running long-lived containers.

To disconnect while allowing the long-lived container to continue running in the background, we use the *-d* or *–detach* switch on the the *docker run* command.

Running a container as detached means that you immediately get your command-line back and the standard output from the container is not redirected to your command-line anymore.

Suppose I want to run a *ping* command. I can use a Linux alpine container for this:

```
docker run alpine ping www.docker.com
```

```
PS C:\> docker run alpine ping www.docker.com
PING www.docker.com (13.32.210.243): 56 data bytes
64 bytes from 13.32.210.243: seq=0 ttl=37 time=7.198 ms
64 bytes from 13.32.210.243: seq=1 ttl=37 time=7.708 ms
64 bytes from 13.32.210.243: seq=2 ttl=37 time=7.015 ms
64 bytes from 13.32.210.243: seq=3 ttl=37 time=7.442 ms
64 bytes from 13.32.210.243: seq=4 ttl=37 time=6.748 ms
64 bytes from 13.32.210.243: seq=5 ttl=37 time=6.743 ms
64 bytes from 13.32.210.243: seq=6 ttl=37 time=6.939 ms
64 bytes from 13.32.210.243: seq=7 ttl=37 time=7.099 ms
64 bytes from 13.32.210.243: seq=8 ttl=37 time=6.674 ms
64 bytes from 13.32.210.243: seq=9 ttl=37 time=7.034 ms
64 bytes from 13.32.210.243: seq=10 ttl=37 time=6.678 ms
```

The ping command doesn't end since it keeps pinging the Docker server. That's a long-lived container. I can detach from it using the *Ctrl-C* shortcut, and it keeps running in the background. But it's best to run it as detached from the beginning:

```
docker run -d alpine ping www.docker.com
```

Note the addition of a *-d* switch. When doing so, the container is started but we don't see its output. Instead, the *docker run* command returns the ID of the container that was just created:

```
PS C:\> docker run -d alpine ping www.docker.com
789b08ce24b1d24fdb077b45cddab30354806e54b3c2d66e9e20e2ab0c542a9a
PS C:\>
```

> The container ID is long. You don't need to write it completely in your commands however. As long as there is no ambiguity, you can use the beginning of the container ID in commands that require the container ID like *docker logs* or *docker run*. That comes very handy when you're managing containers manually.

The container is still running. I can see it using a *docker ps* command that outputs something like:

Container ID	Image	Status
789b08ce24b1	alpine	Up 2 minutes

The status means the container has been running for 2 minutes and is still alive.

I can interact with the running container using commands we saw above: *docker logs* to see its output, *docker inspect* to get detailed information, and even *docker stop* in order to kill it.

Let's look at the standard output of the container using the following command (note I use only the beginning of the container ID):

```
docker logs 789b
```

That prints the whole standard output of the container from its beginning, which may be long. But we can get just a portion of the output using the *–from*, *–until* or *–tail* switches. Let's see the latest 10 seconds of logs for our running container:

```
docker logs --since 10s 789b
```

```
PS C:\> docker logs --since 10s 789b
64 bytes from 13.32.210.219: seq=537 ttl=37 time=6.748 ms
64 bytes from 13.32.210.219: seq=538 ttl=37 time=7.739 ms
64 bytes from 13.32.210.219: seq=539 ttl=37 time=7.450 ms
64 bytes from 13.32.210.219: seq=540 ttl=37 time=7.655 ms
64 bytes from 13.32.210.219: seq=541 ttl=37 time=7.165 ms
64 bytes from 13.32.210.219: seq=542 ttl=37 time=7.495 ms
64 bytes from 13.32.210.219: seq=543 ttl=37 time=12.497 ms
64 bytes from 13.32.210.219: seq=544 ttl=37 time=12.714 ms
64 bytes from 13.32.210.219: seq=545 ttl=37 time=12.051 ms
64 bytes from 13.32.210.219: seq=546 ttl=37 time=6.064 ms
64 bytes from 13.32.210.219: seq=547 ttl=37 time=6.076 ms
PS C:\>
```

> In real-world applications with many running containers you would typically redirect your containers' output to log management services, but anyway it can still be useful to get the last output of a container for debugging purposes.

A long-running container is bound to run for quite some time, but for now I'm going to stop and clean up that container. So I just use:

```
docker stop 789b
docker rm 789b
docker ps -a
```

The last command is just here so that I can check that the container is completely gone.

Listening for incoming network connections

By default a container runs in isolation and as such, it doesn't listen for incoming connections on the machine where it is running. You must explicitly open a port on the host machine and map it to a port on the container.

Suppose I want to run the NGINX web server. It listens for incoming HTTP requests on port 80 by default. If I simply run it, my machine will not route incoming requests to it unless I use the *-p* switch on the *docker run* command.

The *-p* switch takes two parameters: the incoming port you want to open on the host machine, and the port to which it should be mapped inside the container. For instance, here is how I state that I want my machine to listen for incoming connections on port 8085 and route them to port 80 inside a container that runs NGINX:

```
docker run -d -p 8085:80 nginx
```

Note the -d switch. Not mandatory, but since I'm running a server container it's a good idea to keep in the background. An NGINX server container is started and I get its ID:

```
Windows PowerShell                                          —    □    ×
PS C:\> docker run -d -p 8085:80 nginx
8451526dbe11a86979b9eaccc468a9bced0729fdd9f076b96009a4c378c8b7c0
PS C:\>
```

Now I can run a browser and query that server using the http://localhost:8085 URL:

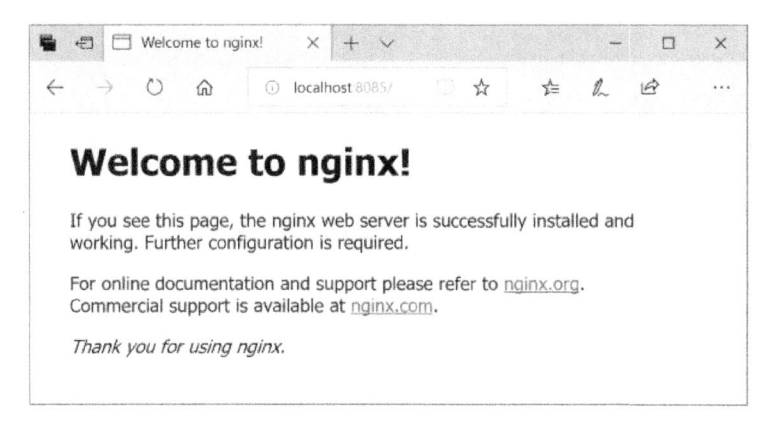

Welcome to nginx!

If you see this page, the nginx web server is successfully installed and working. Further configuration is required.

For online documentation and support please refer to nginx.org.
Commercial support is available at nginx.com.

Thank you for using nginx.

Since that container is running in the background, its output isn't displayed in my terminal. But I can get it using a *docker logs* command:

```
docker logs 8451526dbe11
```

We can see a trace of the browser's HTTP request that NGINX received:

```
PS C:\> docker logs 8451526dbe11
172.17.0.1 - - [02/Jan/2019:09:04:47 +0000] "GET / HTTP/1.1" 200 612 "-" "Mozilla/5.0 (Windows NT 10.0; Win64; x64) AppleWebKit/537.36 (KHTML, like Gecko) Chrome/64.0.3282.140 Safari/537.36 Edge/17.17134" "-"
PS C:\>
```

The NGINX container continues to run and serve incoming requests on port 8085. I can see it using the *docker ps* command. Let's kill it so that I keep my machine free of unused containers:

```
docker stop 8451
docker rm 8451
```

Wrapping it up

Did you notice? We now have the equivalent of getting a brand new server, installing whatever we want on it, and trash it whenever we like.

One thing I particularly like about containers is that they allow me to use any software without polluting my machine. Usually you would hesitate before trying a new piece of software on your machine since it means installing several dependencies that may interfere with existing software and be left over should you change your mind and uninstall the main software. Thanks to containers, I can try even big pieces of server software without polluting my machine.

Let me run a Jenkins server in order to illustrate that point. Jenkins is a full continuous integration server coded using Java. Thanks to Docker I don't need to install Java or any dependency on my machine in order to run a Jenkins server. Jenkins listens by default on port 8080, so I can just go away and type:

```
docker run -p 8088:8080 jenkins
```

> Note that I could add a *-d* switch since this is a long-running process. However, I am not using it here because I want to directly see the verbose output. For a real deployment I would use the *-d* switch and inspect the output with the *docker logs* command when needed.

Then I can point my browser to http://localhost:8088 and finish the setup:

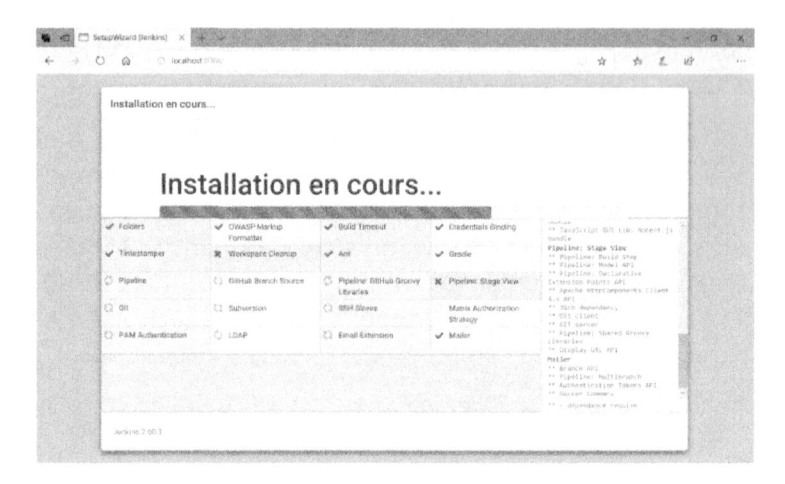

And I get a full-blown Jenkins:

Should I decide not to continue with Jenkins and try another continuous integration server, I can simply run the *docker stop* and *docker rm* commands. I could also run two separate Jenkins server by just executing again the *docker run* command using another port.

Such isolation and ease of use at a very low resource cost is an enormous advantage of containers. Now that you saw how easy it makes managing server software on a single developer machine, imagine how powerful this is going to be on server machines. Thanks to containers, the Ops part of DevOps becomes smooth.

> When using such images, you could wonder about where the data is stored. Docker uses volumes for this, and we'll cover volumes later in this chapter. Also, databases may be needed for storing data, and those may be ran in containers as well. For now, don't worry about that since we need to learn other things first.

4.6 Exercise - Run a server container

> Run a Nextcloud server in a container. The image you need to use is **nextcloud** and it listens by default on port 80.
>
> Make sure you can use the Nextcloud instance with your browser.
>
> Once you're done, stop the container and remove it. Check that the Nextcloud instance is not available anymore in your browser.

More information about the Nextcloud container can be found here[a].

[a] https://hub.docker.com/_/nextcloud

4.7 Exercise solution

- Open a command-line.
- Run the following command:

```
docker run -d -p 8086:80 nextcloud
```

- Take note of the beginning of the container ID that is displayed.
- Open a browser and point it to the following URL:

```
http://localhost:8086
```

- You should see a page that asks you to create an admin account. Input whatever username and password you wish, then click the *Finish install* at the bottom of the page.
- You should see the home screen of Nextcloud. Play around with it as you wish.
- Switch back to the command-line.
- Run the following commands, replacing `<id>` with the container ID you noted earlier:

```
docker stop <id>
docker rm <id>
```

- Switch back to the browser. Check that the application doesn't respond anymore.
- Close the browser.

4.8 Using volumes

When a container writes files, it writes them *inside* of the container. Which means that when the container dies (the host machine restarts, the container is moved from one node to another in a cluster, it simply fails, or many other reasons) all of that data is lost. It also means that if you run several times the same container in a load-balancing scenario, each container will have its own data, which may result in an inconsistent user experience.

A rule of thumb for the sake of simplicity is to ensure that containers are stateless, for instance storing their data in an external database (relational like SQL Server or document-based like MongoDB) or distributed cache (like Redis). But sometimes you actually want to store files in a place where they are persisted. This is done using volumes.

Using a volume, you actually map a directory inside the container to a persistent storage. Persistent storages are manages through drivers and depend on the actual Docker host. They may be an Azure File Storage on Azure, or Amazon S3 on AWS. With Docker Desktop, you can map volumes to actual directories on the host system. This is done using the *-v* switch on the *docker run* command.

Suppose you run a MongoDB database with no volume:

```
docker run -d mongo
```

Any data stored in that database will be lost when the container is stopped or restarted. In order to avoid data loss, you can use a volume mount:

```
docker run -v /your/dir:/data/db -d mongo
```

It will ensure that any data written to the */data/db* directory inside the container is actually written to the */your/dir* on the host system. Hence that data is kept when the container is restarted.

4.9 Where do images come from?

Each container is created from an image. You provide the image name to the *docker run* command. Docker first looks for the image locally, and uses it when present. When the image is not present locally, it is downloaded from a *registry*.

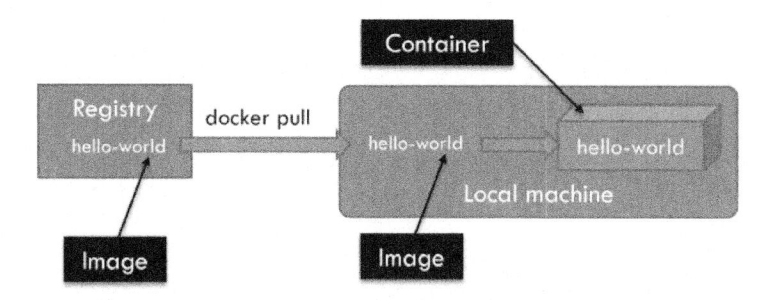

> You can list the local images using the following command: *docker images ls*.

When an image is published to a registry, its name must be:

`<repository_name>/<name>:<tag>>`

- *tag* is optional. When missing, it is considered to be *latest*
- *repository_name* may be a registry DNS or the name of a registry in the Docker Hub.

We'll soon see more about Docker Hub and private registries. All of the images we've been using now were downloaded from Docker Hub since they are not DNS names. The Docker Hub may be browsed here[1].

For instance, the Jenkins image may be found here[2] on the Docker Hub.

Although the *docker run* command downloads images automatically when missing, you may want to manually trigger the download. You can simply use the *docker pull* command. A pull command will force a download of an image, whether it is already present or not.

---
[1] https://hub.docker.com/
[2] https://hub.docker.com/_/jenkins

Some scenarios where using a *docker pull* command is relevant:

- you expect that the machine that will run the containers will not have access to the registries (e.g. no internet connection) at the time of running the containers;
- you want the ensure you have the latest version of an image tagged as "latest", which wouldn't be downloaded by the *docker run* command.

5. Create Docker images

As we saw earlier, containers are created from images. Up to now we've been using images created by others. It's high time we learnt how to create our own images. Inside our images we can stuff our programs and their dependencies, so that many containers can be created from those images and live happily ever after.

5.1 Creating a simple image

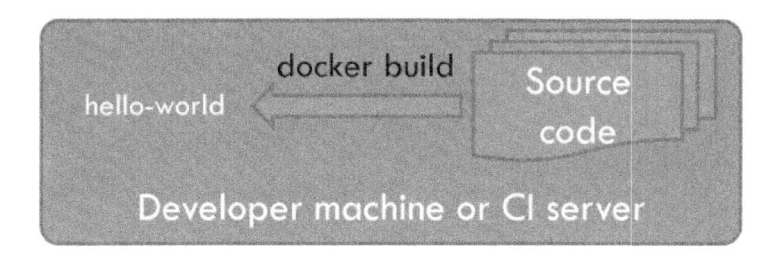

A Docker image is created using the *docker build* command and a *Dockerfile* file. The *Dockerfile* file contains instructions that state how the image should be built.

> The *Dockerfile* file can have any name. Naming it *Dockerfile* makes it easier for others to understand its purpose when they see that file in your project, and means we don't need to state the file name when using the *docker build* command.

I'd like to create a basic image for a container that displays a "hello world" message when ran.

For this, I create a file named *Dockerfile* that describes how my image should be built. A *Dockerfile* file always begins with a *FROM* instruction because an image is based on another base image. This is a powerful feature since it allows you to extend images that may already be complex.

For my simple text output need, I may use a Debian Linux image. Here's my *Dockerfile* file:

```
FROM debian:8
```

This is not enough. I really get a Debian Linux basis but I do not run any command that could display "hello world". This can be achieved using the *CMD* instruction. The *CMD* instruction states which executable is ran when a container is created using your image, and provides optional arguments.

Here's an improved *Dockerfile* file that creates a Debian Linux-based image and instructs it to greet our users when a container spawns:

Dockerfile

```
FROM debian:8

CMD ["echo", "Hello world"]
```

Note that the program to be ran and its arguments are provided as a JSON array of strings.

In order to create an image from my *Dockerfile* file, I need to run the *docker build* command. So I type the following command in my terminal, in the folder where the *Dockerfile* file lives:

```
docker build -t hello .
```

The -t switch is used in front of the desired image. Indeed, an image may be created without a name (it would have only a generated unique ID) so it is an optional parameter on the *docker build* command.

> Note the dot at the end of the command above. It states which path is used as the build context (more about that later), and where the *Dockerfile* is expected to be found. Should my *Dockerfile* have another name or live elsewhere, I can add a -f switch in order to provide the file path.

The *docker build* command just created an image named *hello*. That image is stored locally on my computer, and I can run it as I would run any other image:

```
docker run --rm hello
```

As expected, the *docker run* command above simply prints the message:

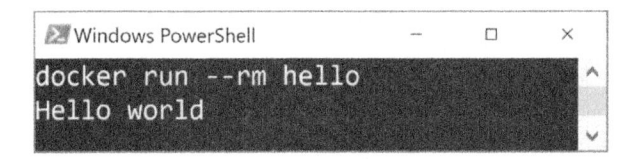

```
docker run --rm hello
Hello world
```

From there, you may want to publish your image for others to run containers based on it. We'll see how to do that in the Publish Docker images chapter but for now I want to tell you more about creating images.

Just to make things crystal clear, here's what I did:

- create an image:
  - create a file named *Dockerfile*
  - run a *docker build* command
- run a container from the image created.

I'd like to insist again on what this means: running a container is the virtual equivalent of starting a brand new machine then trashing it. I mean, in order to print that "Hello world" message we virtually got a new computer, had it execute an *echo* command, then trashed it. Docker makes fire-and-forget computing cheap. Of course, this is complete overkill for such a simple purpose, but it will remain true even when we install frameworks or move files around inside our containers: it's a fantastic feature and most of your Docker power will come when you understand how easily you can create and trash isolated virtual computers.

5.2 Creating an image including files

The image we just created didn't need anything more than what the base image already contained, which is why our *Dockerfile* file was so simple. In a real world scenario however I'm very likely to want files to be part of an image I create.

Suppose I have a file named *index.html* on my disk with the following contents:

index.html

```
<html>
  <body>
    <h1>Hello !</h1>
    <div>I'm hosted by a container.</div>
  </body>
</html>
```

I'd like to create an image that includes a web server that will serve this page over HTTP. NGINX is a good candidate. I could keep using the *debian* base image and add instructions to my *Dockerfile* file that install NGINX, but it's easier to base my work on images that were already configured and tested. The Docker Hub contains an NGINX image[1] where NGINX was already installed with a configuration that serves files found in the */usr/share/nginx/html* directory.

I create the following *Dockerfile* file in the same folder as the HTML file:

Dockerfile
```
FROM nginx:1.15

COPY index.html /usr/share/nginx/html
```

Apart from the *nginx* base image, you can see a *COPY* instruction. Its first parameter is the file to be copied from the build context and second is the destination directory inside the image.

The build context is basically the directory you provide to the *docker build* command. Its contents are available for *COPY* instructions to use, but only during the image build process. That means it's available only for the instructions in the *Dockerfile* file, and files from it won't be part of the build image (and containers that you'll spawn from that image) unless you use the *COPY* instruction. Which is why we have a *COPY* instruction: we want the *index.html* file to be part of the */usr/share/nginx/html* directory inside the image we create.

---
[1] https://hub.docker.com/_/nginx

You may have noticed that this time the *Dockerfile* file contains no *CMD* instruction. Remember that the *CMD* instruction states which executable should be ran when a container is created from my image, so it's weird that I don't include a *CMD* instruction that runs an NGINX server. Right. The reason why I didn't include a *CMD* instruction is because the base *nginx:1.15* image already contains such a *CMD* instruction to run the NGINX server, so it's part of my image and I don't need to include my own *CMD* instruction as long as I don't want to run *another* executable on container startup.

Back to creating our HTTP server image, I open a command line inside the folder where my *index.html* and *Dockerfile* files are, and run the following commands:

Dockerfile

```
docker build -t webserver .
docker run --rm -it -p 8082:80 webserver
```

Those commands build a *webserver* from the *Dockerfile* file instructions, then start a container that listens to my machine's 8082 port and redirect the incoming connections to the container's 80 port. I can start a browser and point it to *http://localhost:8082*. That displays the HTML file contents in my browser, since they are served over HTTP by the running container:

> **Hello !**
>
> I'm hosted by a container.

In the command-line I can see a log from NGINX that proves it received the HTTP request from my browser:

```
172.17.0.1 - - [.../2019:21:14:46 +0000] "GET / HTTP/1.\
1" 304 0 "-" "..." "-"
```

When running my container I added the *–rm* and *-it* switches simply for demo purposes. In real life that server container would be long running so I'd run it without those switches. Here's why I used the switches:

- the *-it* switch allows me to stop the container using *Ctrl-C* from the command-line;
- the *–rm* switch ensures that the container is deleted once it has stopped.

5.3 Images are created locally

When I run the *docker build* command in order to create an image from a *Dockerfile* file, the resulting image is stored locally on the computer where the *docker build* command is ran.

This allows me to run as many containers as I want from the locally created image, but chances are that I want other computers to be able to run containers from the image I created. We'll learn how to do that in the next chapter.

I can see the images available locally on my computer by running the following command:

```
docker image ls
```

Taking into account the images I built earlier, I can see something along those lines:

REPOSITORY	TAG	IMAGE ID
webserver	latest	c067edac5ec1
hello	latest	347c4eed84cd
nginx	1.15	f09fe80eb0e7
debian	8	ec0727c65ed3

Having the images readily available locally makes it fast to run a container from them. However, there will be a time when some images are useless. I can remove them from my local machine using the *docker rmi* command and providing it the image name or image ID.

For instance, I could remove the *webserver:latest* image using any of the following two commands:

```
docker rmi c067edac5ec1
docker rmi webserver:latest
```

5.4 Exercise - Build an image and run it

*Create a file named *compute.js* with the following code that computes and displays the area of a disk using JavaScript:*

```
var radius = 2.0;
var area = Math.pow(radius, 2) * Math.PI;
console.log(
    `Area of a ${radius} cm circle:
    ${area} cm² `
);
```

*Create a Docker image that runs this code using the *node:11-alpine* image that contains Node.JS. The command that runs a JavaScript program using Node.JS is* node <filename>.

> You may find the source code for the *compute.js* file in the *create-docker-images/exercises/jsimage/starter* folder, and the source code for the solution in the *create-docker-images/exercises/jsimage/solution* folder.

5.5 Exercise solution

- Create a file named *Dockerfile* and add the following code to it:

```
FROM node:11-alpine

COPY compute.js .

CMD node compute.js
```

- Open a command-line. Change the current directory to the directory where you created the *Dockerfile* and the *compute.js* file.
- Run the following command:

```
docker build -t jsimage .
```

- Once the image has been built, run the following command:

```
docker run --rm jsimage
```

- You can see an output similar to that one:

```
PS C:\> docker run --rm jsimage
Area of a 2 cm circle:
    12.566370614359172 cm²
PS C:\>
```

5.6 Tags matter

We saw earlier that image names include a name and tag. As a quick reminder about this, an image name is:

```
<repository_name>/<name>:<tag>
```

- *tag* is optional. When missing, it is considered to be *latest*

- *repository_name* may be a registry DNS or the name of a registry in the Docker Hub.

While your images aren't published to a registry (which is what we do in this chapter, but that will change in the next one) you don't need to include a registry name. So your image name is:

```
<name>:<tag>
```

The *latest* tag

In my demonstrations I didn't include a tag, hence the default *latest* tag was used. For instance, the actual image name was *hello:latest* when I ran the following command:

```
docker build -t hello .
```

As long as you are creating simple software, running on a simple CI/CD pipeline, it can be fine to use the *latest* tag. In a simple scenario, you may:

1. update the source code;
2. build a new image with the *latest* tag;
3. run a new container with the newest image;
4. kill the previous container.

There's a caveat with this however: when using the *docker run hello* command on a distant machine (which actually means *docker run hello:**latest***), the distant machine has no means to know that there is a newer version of the *hello:latest* image, so you need to run the *docker pull hello* on the distant machine in order for the newest version of your image to be downloaded to that machine.

This may sound awkward an that's one reason for not just using the *latest* tag.

Why would you tag your images?

Other reasons soon come once you become more serious with your CI/CD pipeline. For instance, you may want any or all of the following features:

- be able to rollback to a previous version if you detect a problem with the latest image;
- run different versions in different environments, for instance the latest version in a test environment and the previous version in a production environment;
- run different versions at the same time, routing some users to the latest version and some to the previous versions (known as canary release);
- deploy different versions to different users, and be able to run whatever version on your development machine while you support them.

Those are all good reasons for tagging your images. If you ensure each released image has a different tag, you can run any of the scenarios mentioned above.

You're free to tag your images however you want. Common tags include:

- a version number, e.g. *hello:1.0*, *hello:1.1*, *hello:1.2*
- a Git commit tag, e.g. *hello:2cd7e376*, *hello:b43a14bb*

In order to apply a tag, just state it during your build command:

```
docker build -t hello:1.0 .
```

Tags for base images

Remember your images are based on other images. This is done using the *FROM* instruction in your *Dockerfile* file. Just as you can tag your images, the base image you use may be the *latest* one or a tagged one.

In my demos I used tagged images. For instance, I based my server image on the *nginx:1.15* base image. It's quite tempting to base your images on the latest ones so that you're always running on up-to-date software, especially since it's very easy: all you need to do is omit the tag or state the *latest* one. So you could be tempted to use the following instruction in your *Dockerfile* file:

```
FROM nginx:latest
```

Don't. First, it doesn't mean that any container running will be based on the latest available version of the *nginx* image. Docker is about having reproducible image, so the *latest* version is evaluated when you build your image, not when the container is ran. It means that the version will not change unless you run the *docker build* command again.

Second, you're likely to run into trouble. What about the *nginx* image releasing a new version with breaking changes? If you build your image again, you're likely to get a broken image.

For these reasons, I recommend specifying the image tag. If you want to keep up to date with new releases of the base image, update the tag manually and make sure you test your image before releasing it.

5.7 Parameters as environment variables

In real life, a container's inputs and outputs are likely to vary according to its environment. For instance, if you run a web application it is likely to connect to a database and listen for incoming requests on a given DNS. The database connection details and DNS will have different values on a development machine, on the test server and the production server.

Reading a value

Whatever the technology you use inside your container, you can access environment variables. For instance, if you set a *name* environment variable, you may access it with:

Technology	Access
Linux shell	$name
.NET Core	.AddEnvironmentVariables();
Java	System.getenv("name")
Node.JS	process.env.name
PHP	.$_ENV["name"]
Python	os.environ.get('name')

Providing a value

On a real machine, environment variables are set on your system. Inside a container, they can be set from several sources, which make them appropriate for parameterizing your containers.

In order to provide an environment variable's value at runtime, you simply use the *-e name=value* parameter on the *docker run* command.

> A special use case is when the system that runs the container has the *name* environment variable defined and you want to reuse it, then you can simply

> use the -e *name* parameter without specifying a value.

Default value

You may also want to define a default value for an environment variable, in case it isn't provided when a container is created. This may be done in the *Dockerfile* file, using the *ENV* instruction. For instance, the following will make sure that if the *name* variable isn't provided to the *docker run* command it will have a default value of *Dockie*:

```
ENV name=Dockie
```

It's good practice to add a *ENV* instruction for every environment variable your image expects, since it documents your image.

Sample usage

I want to create an image that can ping any given site. I'll do this using a Linux shell script. I define it in a *ping.sh* file:

ping.sh

```
#!/bin/sh

echo "Pinging $host..."
ping -c 5 $host
```

Note that I make use of a *host* environment variable. I'm going to define an image that includes and runs that script:

Dockerfile

```
FROM debian:8

ENV host=www.google.com

COPY ping.sh .

CMD ["sh", "ping.sh"]
```

Note that my *Dockerfile* file includes an *ENV* instruction that specifies that the *host* variable will be *www.google.com* in case it isn't provided. I create my image from that *Dockerfile* file by running a *docker build* command:

```
docker build -t pinger .
```

Next, I run two containers based on that image:

```
docker run --rm pinger
docker run --rm -e host=www.bing.com pinger
```

The first one isn't provided any value for the *host* environment variable so it defaults to the *www.google.com* value specified in the *Dockerfile* file. The second container is provided the *www.bing.com* value. Here's the output from those two containers (shortened for brevity):

```
C:\>docker run --rm pinger
Pinging www.google.com...
PING www.google.com (172.217.18.196) 56(84) bytes of da\
ta.
64 bytes from par10s38-in-f4.1e100.net (172.217.18.196)\
 : icmp_seq=1 ttl=37 time=6.52 ms
[...]
64 bytes from par10s38-in-f4.1e100.net (172.217.18.196)\
 : icmp_seq=5 ttl=37 time=7.35 ms

--- www.google.com ping statistics ---
5 packets transmitted, 5 received, 0% packet loss, time\
 4005ms
rtt min/avg/max/mdev = 5.632/7.854/11.031/1.890 ms

C:\>docker run --rm -e host=www.bing.com pinger
Pinging www.bing.com...
PING dual-a-0001.a-msedge.net (204.79.197.200) 56(84) b\
ytes of data.
64 bytes from a-0001.a-msedge.net (204.79.197.200): icm\
p_seq=1 ttl=37 time=7.82 ms
[...]
```

```
64 bytes from a-0001.a-msedge.net (204.79.197.200): icm\
p_seq=5 ttl=37 time=8.08 ms

--- dual-a-0001.a-msedge.net ping statistics ---
5 packets transmitted, 5 received, 0% packet loss, time\
 4005ms
rtt min/avg/max/mdev = 7.820/8.669/10.193/0.954 ms
```

You can see that each container pinged a different host, according to the values provided to them.

This was a simple demo, but you can provide advanced values. You would typically provide full connection strings, URLs to other services, usernames and passwords and so on. This is a flexible and powerful feature since those values may come from many sources once you begin to use orchestrators.

5.8 Exercise - Enable an image to be parameterized

In the *create-docker-images/exercises/js-param/starter* folder you'll find a *compute.js* file with the following code:

```
var radius = process.env.diameter / 2;
var area = Math.pow(radius, 2) * Math.PI;
console.log(
    `Area of a ${radius} cm radius disk:
    ${area} cm²`
);
```

> It's a modified version of the code from the previous exercises. It expects a *diameter* environment variable to be available and displays the area of a disk for that given diameter. Create a Docker image that runs this code using the *node:11-alpine* image that contains Node.JS. Run two containers with different values for the diameter.

The source code for the solution can be found in the *create-docker-images/exercises/jsparam/solution* folder.

5.9 Exercise solution

- Create a file named *Dockerfile* and add the following code to it:

```
FROM node:11-alpine

ENV diameter=4.0

COPY compute.js .

CMD node compute.js
```

- Open a command-line. Change the current directory to the directory where you created the *Dockerfile* and the *compute.js* file.
- Run the following command:

```
docker build -t jsparam .
```

- Once the image has been built, run the following commands:

```
docker run --rm jsparam
docker run --rm -e diameter=5.0 jsparam
```

- You can see an output similar to that one:

```
C:\>docker run --rm jsparam
Area of a 2 cm radius disk:
    12.566370614359172 cm2


C:\>docker run --rm -e diameter=5.0 jsparam
Area of a 2.5 cm radius disk:
    19.634954084936208 cm2
```

5.10 Storage

As we saw in the Using volumes chapter you'd better create images that result in stateless containers that rely on external data stores. Sometimes however you need to store your data in a persistent file system.

When this need arises, use the *VOLUME* instruction as such:

```
VOLUME /path/to/directory
```

The */path/to/directory* is a path to a directory used inside the image. When a container is created using the *docker run* command, the *-v* switch may be used in order to map this directory to an actual volume on the host system.

This is only an indication. By default, if the user doesn't map this volume to an external store for the container, the data will be stored inside the container.

5.11 Networking

When your image hosts server software, it listens on one or several ports. For instance, an HTTP server generally listens on the TCP port 80.

You can explicit this using an *EXPOSE* instruction:

EXPOSE 80

Using this instruction is purely for documentation purposes. Indeed, it will NOT open that port to the outside world when a container is created from that image. Anyone who creates a container will need to explicitly bind that port to an actual port of the host machine using the *-p* switch of the *docker run* command. In case you forgot, this is what we saw in the Listening for incoming network connections chapter.

Why use the *EXPOSE* instruction then? Again, it is only for documentation purposes: it enables someone who wants to run a container from your image to know which ports they should redirect to the outside world using the *-p* switch of the *docker run* command.

5.12 Learning more

Docker maintains a reference of the instructions you can use in a *Dockerfile* file. You can find it here[2].

[2]https://docs.docker.com/engine/reference/builder/

6. Publish Docker images

6.1 Rationale for publishing

When you create a container, you create it from an image that is available on your machine:

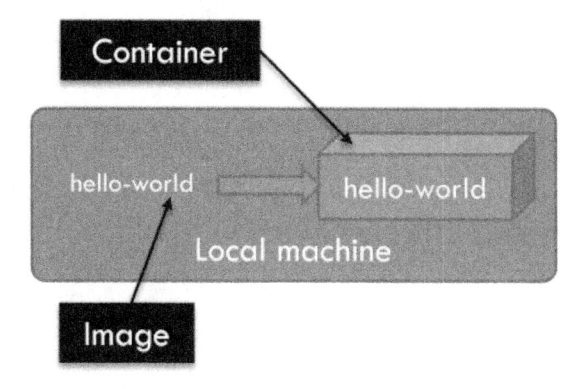

There are two ways to have an image available on your machine:

- create an image using the *docker build* command: we saw this in the previous chapter;

- get an image from a Registry, using the *docker pull* command or implicitly when using the *docker run* command for an image that is not available locally.

Here's what happens when you create a container from an image that is pulled from a registry:

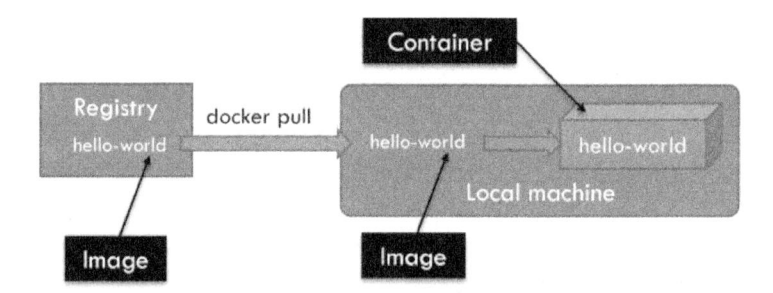

As a developer, you create images for your software to run in a controlled environment. Since you want your images to run on other machines, you need to make sure they are distributed to those machines. Your option for this is simply to publish your images to a Registry. When the other machines need to create containers from your images, they will simply pull them from the Registry.

In other words, when you want to publish your application to test or to put on a production environment, you simply upload your image to a Registry.

6.2 Registries

A Docker Registry is basically an image store that offers the following functions:

- ability to store various images;
- ability to store various tags for the same image;
- an HTTP API that allows to push images from a machine that produces them, or pull images to a machine that runs containers from those images;
- TLS-secured connection to the API in order to avoid man-in-the-middle attacks.

There are many registries available. You can use the publicly available Docker Hub (following chapter) or use a private registry of your own. There are many ways to create private registries, and we'll cover several of them in the *Private registries* chapter. In any case, the process to tag and publish your images remains the same on every registry.

6.3 Publishing an image

Whatever the Registry you choose, publishing an image is a three-step process:

1. build your image (*docker build*) with the appropriate prefix name or tag (*docker tag*) an existing one appropriately;

2. log into the Registry (*docker login*);
3. push the image into the Registry (*docker push*).

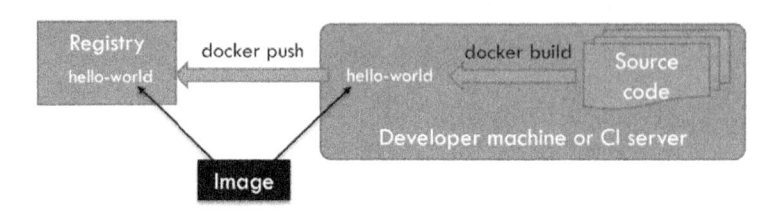

There are slight variations according to the actual Registry, which we'll see in the following chapters.

6.4 Docker Hub

Docker Hub is a Docker Registry offered by Docker Inc. It allows unlimited storage of public images, and paid plans to host your private images. A public image may be accessed by others, which is exactly what you want when you make your software widely available - less for internal enterprise software.

In order to publish images on Docker Hub you need to create an account. I'm going to create one. For this, I head to https://hub.docker.com/ and click the *Sign Up* link. The *Docker ID* I select will be the prefix of images I publish to the Docker Hub.

When creating your account make sure you select the right ID since it will be part of your images' names. Suppose your ID name is *short-name*, your images should be tagged:

```
<short_name>/<name>:<tag>
```

For this book I created the *learnbook* account, and I want to publish the *webserver* image I created earlier. It's as simple as naming it correctly and pushing it to the Registry. I need to name it *learnbook/webserver*, and there are two ways to do this.

First is to run the *docker build* command again using the correct name. That's a good option when you're using it from the start, but if I do this now it will result in two separate images on my disk - same contents but different names and IDs. Not a good idea.

My second option is much better: use the *docker tag* command. A Docker image can have several names as needed, and they can all be added to an already existing image thanks to the *docker tag* command. The *docker tag* doesn't duplicate the image (contrary to running *docker build* again).

The *docker tag* command accepts two arguments: first the name of an existing image, second the name you want to add to that image.

```
docker tag webserver learnbook/webserver
```

I now have a single Docker image known by my machine under two names: *webserver* and *short_name/webserver*.

In case I run the *docker image ls* command, it will appear as two separate lines:

REPOSITORY	TAG	IMAGE ID
short_name / webserver	latest	c067edac5ec1
webserver	latest	c067edac5ec1

Note that the *image ID* is the same for both lines, which means there really is just one image on my machine, known under different names.

Now that my image is named correctly, I can publish it to the Docker hub. It's just a matter of running two commands:

```
docker login
docker push learnbook/webserver
```

> The *docker login* command asks for my Docker Hub credentials interactively, but I could have just as well provided them as arguments to the command.

The *docker push* command is smart enough to push only the bits that differ from the base *nginx* image I used since it is already stored in the Docker Hub, as the output shows:

```
The push refers to repository [docker.io/learnbook/webs\
erver]
0f83d7865e1e: Pushed
6b5e2ed60418: Mounted from library/nginx
92c15149e23b: Mounted from library/nginx
0a07e81f5da3: Mounted from library/nginx
latest: digest: sha256:e8597...1ae0b1efb1 size: 1155
```

That's it! The Docker Hub now hosts my image for everyone to see and run it.

> Everyone can see my image because it is public. In case I don't want to share it with the whole world, I can set it as private.

6.5 Run an image on another machine

This is an extremely easy process. In fact you already know how: use the *docker run* command. Or first get the image with *docker pull* then use it with *docker run* (this would be useful in case you plan to disconnect from the internet before running a container, for instance).

In fact, you can try it on your machine (with *Docker Engine* or *Docker Desktop* installed). Run the following command:

```
docker run --rm -it -p 8085:80 learnbook/webserver
```

Then pop-up your browser and head on to the following URL in order to see my web page being served over HTTP by that container.

```
http://localhost:8085
```

Isn't that neat? A painless delivery system.

> There's a little variant to this. In case you want to run an image that is stored in a private registry, you first need to log into the registry using the *docker login* command. Once this is done, you can *docker pull* the image. Should you want to run another container with that image later on, you don't need to login since the image is stored on your machine.

6.6 Exercise - Publish an image and run a container on another machine

Create a Docker ID on https://hub.docker.com/

Publish your *jsparam* image to the Docker Hub.

Get another machine that runs *Docker Engine* or *Docker Desktop* and create two containers from the published *jsparam* image in order to compute the area of circles that have diameters of 3.5 cm and 1.5 cm.

6.7 Exercise solution

- Head to https://hub.docker.com/ with a browser and click the *Sign Up* link.
- Create an account with the *Docker ID* you wish (in the rest if this solution we'll suppose it is *learnbook*, but replace it with your own).
- Open a command-line.
- Run the following commands:

```
docker tag jsparam learnbook/jsparam
docker login -u learnbook -p <your-password>
docker push learnbook/jsparam
```

- Get another machine that runs *Docker Engine* or *Docker Desktop* and open a command-line.
- Run the following commands:

```
docker run --rm -e diameter=3.5 learnbook/jsparam
docker run --rm -e diameter=1.5 learnbook/jsparam
```

You should get the following output:

```
> docker run --rm -e diameter=3.5 learnbook/jsparam
Unable to find image 'learnbook/jsparam:latest' locally
latest: Pulling from learnbook/jsparam
Digest: sha256:a80621fe...328f3
Status: Downloaded newer image for learnbook/jsparam:la\
test
Area of a 1.75 cm radius disk:
    9.62112750161874 cmÂ²

> docker run --rm -e diameter=1.5 learnbook/jsparam
Area of a 0.75 cm radius disk:
    1.7671458676442586 cmÂ²
```

6.8 Private registries

Public registries are a convenient way to share your Docker images, but you will probably want to keep some images to your company, yourself or an organization. Private registries ensure you can keep your private images... private.

When we published our images to the Docker Hub using the *docker push* command, we had to use the *docker login* command first in order to authenticate. A private registry will require users to also use *docker login* before they can pull an image.

There are many ways to get a private registry:

- Docker Hub, where you pay according to the quantity of private repositories used;
- Azure Container Registry allows you to have your own private registry in Azure;
- GitLab has an included optional Docker registry: enable it so that each project can store the images it creates;
- The registry[1] image allows you to host your own registry on a Docker enabled machine as a container.

Storing images in a private registry is the same process we used when pushing images to the Docker Hub: your

---
[1] https://hub.docker.com/_/registry

images' names simply need to be prefixed with the registry name before they are pushed.

6.9 Size matters

When you create an image, you want it to be as small as possible for several reasons:

- reduce pull and push times;
- use a minimum amount of space in the Registry;
- use a minimum amount of space on the machines that will run the containers;
- use a minimum amount of space on the machine that creates the image.

In order to reduce the size of an image, you need to understand that it is influenced by several factors:

- the files included in your image;
- the base image size;
- image layers.

Ideally you want to reduce those. Let's see how.

Files included in your image

Include only necessary files in your image. That may sound obvious, but it's easy to include unwanted files.

First of all, avoid *COPY* instructions with wildcards. A typical example that should be avoided is:

```
COPY . .
```

Try to be specific, if necessary splitting them into various *COPY* instructions like:

```
COPY ./Project/src/*.ts ./src
COPY ./Project/package.json .
```

Obviously you will need to use *COPY* instructions that copy whole folders, for instance:

```
COPY ./js/built /app/js
```

However, you may want to exclude files from that copy. You can use a *.dockerignore* file for that purpose. Simply add a *.dockerignore* file at the root of your build context that lists files and folders that should be excluded from the build like a *.gitignore* file.

Here is an example *.dockerignore* file:

```
# Ignore .git folder
.git
# Ignore Typescript files in any folder or subfolder
**/*.ts
```

Second, when using package managers like NPM, NuGet, apt and so on, make sure you run them while building the image. It will avoid sending them as the context of the image, and it will allow the layer caching system to cache the result of running them. As long as the definition file doesn't change, Docker will reuse its cache.

Base image size

The base image you choose in your *FROM* instruction (the one at the top of your *Dockerfile* file) is part of the image you build.

There are optimizations in which a machine will not pull the base image when pulling your image, as long as it already pulled that base image before. But oftentimes such optimizations cannot be ran, so you'd better reference small base images.

Many images that you can use as base images have smaller variants. For instance, the *debian* image I used in the *Create Docker images* chapter is quite big. Here is the definition I used:

Dockerfile

```
FROM debian:8

CMD ["echo", "Hello world"]
```

That definition results in an image that weights 127 MB (size can be checked using the *docker image ls* command).

If I head to the description page[2] of that image, I can see that there is a smaller variant using the *8-slim* tag. Here is an optimized definition:

---

[2]https://hub.docker.com/_/debian

Dockerfile

```
FROM debian:8-slim

CMD ["echo", "Hello world"]
```

That revised definition yields an image that weights 79.3 MB. We just saved 38% of the original image size.

The same can be done using a *node:alpine* image instead of the default *node* image. For instance, the image definition I used for my *webserver* image results in a 109 MB image:

Dockerfile

```
FROM nginx:1.15

COPY index.html /usr/share/nginx/html
```

If I switch the base image from *nginx:1.15* to *nginx:1.15-alpine*, the resulting image weights only 16.1 MB. That's a 85% saving over the original image size! Here's the optimized image definition:

Dockerfile

```
FROM nginx:1.15-alpine

COPY index.html /usr/share/nginx/html
```

Image layers

When creating an image, Docker reads each instruction in order and the resulting partial image is kept separate: it is cached and labeled with a unique ID. Such caching is very effective because it is used at different moments of an image life:

- in a future build, Docker will use the cached part instead of recreating it as long as it is possible;
- when pushing a new version of the image to a Registry, the common part is not pushed;
- when pulling an image from a registry, the common part you already have is not pulled.

The caching mechanism can be summed up as follows: when building a new image Docker will try its best to skip all instructions up to the first instruction that actually changes the resulting image. All prior instructions result in the cached layers being used. Let's see some examples.

Suppose I want to create an image that included PHP, so I create the following *Dockerfile* file:

```
FROM debian:8

COPY . .

RUN apt-get update && apt-get upgrade && apt-get dist-u\
pgrade -y
RUN apt-get install -y php5
```

When I build it using the *docker build* command, it takes quite some time because the two *RUN* steps need to download files and manipulate them. That's normal and expected. Here's the truncated output:

```
Step 1/4 : FROM debian:8
 ---> ec0727c65ed3
Step 2/4 : COPY . .
 ---> cb8153c1f09a
Step 3/4 : RUN apt-get update && apt-get upgrade && apt\
-get dist-upgrade -y
 ---> Running in eff335d4aeba
Get:1 http://security.debian.org jessie/updates InRelea\
se [44.9 kB][...]
[...]
Removing intermediate container eff335d4aeba
 ---> f4a652ba0849
Step 4/4 : RUN apt-get install -y php5
 ---> Running in d43a7a64606d
Reading package lists...
Building dependency tree...
Reading state information...
The following extra packages will be installed:
```

```
  apache2 apache2-bin apache2-data apache2-utils file i\
fupdown isc-dhcp-client
  isc-dhcp-common krb5-locales libalgorithm-c3-perl lib\
apache2-mod-php5
[...]
Need to get 23.2 MB of archives.
After this operation, 88.3 MB of additional disk space \
will be used.
Get:1 http://deb.debian.org/debian/ jessie/main libgdbm\
3 amd64 1.8.3-13.1 [30.0 kB]
Get:2 http://deb.debian.org/debian/ jessie/main libjson\
-c2 amd64 0.11-4 [24.8 kB]
[...]
Preparing to unpack .../libkrb5support0_1.12.1+dfsg-19+\
deb8u5_amd64.deb ...
Unpacking libkrb5support0:amd64 (1.12.1+dfsg-19+deb8u5)\

  ...
Selecting previously unselected package libk5crypto3:am\
d64.
[...]
Removing intermediate container d43a7a64606d
 ---> 3499256d8527
Successfully built 3499256d8527
```

Since this is the first build, each instruction is processed. Each of the 4 steps has been cached however.

If I run the same *docker build* command without changing anything, I can benefit from the cached layers. The whole build process takes less than a second and here's the output:

```
Step 1/4 : FROM debian:8
 ---> ec0727c65ed3
Step 2/4 : COPY . .
 ---> Using cache
 ---> cb8153c1f09a
Step 3/4 : RUN apt-get update && apt-get upgrade && apt\
-get dist-upgrade -y
 ---> Using cache
 ---> f4a652ba0849
Step 4/4 : RUN apt-get install -y php5
 ---> Using cache
 ---> 3499256d8527
Successfully built 3499256d8527
```

Note that each layer ID matches the ID of a layer that has been cache previously. For instance, the *apt-get update* command created the *5fa6ecc854bb* layer, and running the same command gets us the same layer. If I had pushed the previous image to a Registry and I would push that one, almost nothing would actually be pushed.

That's efficient but unreal. In real life I would rebuild my image because some of the files used in the *COPY* step changed. Let's change a file in the current directory and run the exact same *docker build* command. We can painfully see that the cache isn't used and the build process takes several seconds again because it needs to download, unpack and install all the packages:

```
Step 1/4 : FROM debian:8
 ---> ec0727c65ed3
Step 2/4 : COPY . .
 ---> edec0c4e4746
Step 3/4 : RUN apt-get update && apt-get upgrade && apt\
-get dist-upgrade -y
 ---> Running in ddc4ad55ab7d
Ign http://deb.debian.org jessie InRelease
Get:1 http://deb.debian.org jessie-updates InRelease [1\
45 kB]
Get:2 http://security.debian.org jessie/updates InRelea\
se [44.9 kB]
[...]
Removing intermediate container ddc4ad55ab7d
 ---> 6d484f51c8f8
Step 4/4 : RUN apt-get install -y php5
 ---> Running in b6ba3afb3cc9
Reading package lists...
Need to get 23.2 MB of archives.
After this operation, 88.3 MB of additional disk space \
will be used.
[...]
Removing intermediate container b6ba3afb3cc9
 ---> 48c3c3bf2fad
Successfully built 48c3c3bf2fad
```

Why wasn't any cache used this time? Simply because the *COPY* instruction was impacted by our changing a file. If we push that image to a Registry, the whole image will be pushed since no cache was used.

How can we improve this? Simply by changing the order

of the instructions in the *Dockerfile* file. Indeed, the files copied by the *COPY* instruction are much more likely to change than the packages needed to install PHP5. So we can first install PHP and then copy the files. Here's the improved *Dockerfile* file:

```
FROM debian:8

RUN apt-get update && apt-get upgrade && apt-get dist-u\
pgrade -y
RUN apt-get install -y php5

COPY . .
```

Note that the *COPY* instruction has been placed last. That's the only change.

If I run the *docker build* instruction, then change some files in the folder (as we did earlier), and run the *docker build* command again, here's what we get. On the first *docker build*, the whole build is done, taking up several seconds:

```
Step 1/4 : FROM debian:8
 ---> ec0727c65ed3
Step 2/4 : RUN apt-get update && apt-get upgrade && apt\
-get dist-upgrade -y
[...]
 ---> 219277a22ec2
Step 3/4 : RUN apt-get install -y php5
[...]
 ---> e493f018171f
Step 4/4 : COPY . .
[...]
 ---> 5d1f58a397c7
Successfully built 5d1f58a397c7
```

Now, if I change a file and run the *docker build* command again, the whole process only takes a few seconds because cached layers are used for everything except the *COPY* instruction:

```
Step 1/4 : FROM debian:8
 ---> ec0727c65ed3
Step 2/4 : RUN apt-get update && apt-get upgrade && apt\
-get dist-upgrade -y
 ---> Using cache
 ---> 219277a22ec2
Step 3/4 : RUN apt-get install -y php5
 ---> Using cache
 ---> e493f018171f
Step 4/4 : COPY . .
 ---> 08c87dcf7267
Successfully built 08c87dcf7267
```

Note how the ID of the layers resulting from step 1 to 3 are the same. Only step 4 produces a different layer.

As you can see, we had the exact same instructions in both case. The only change was the order of those instructions, which yielded a fantastic boost. In order to benefit from caching, do the steps in the *Dockerfile* that are likely to change, or have their input change, as late as possible.

7. Forget SDK installs

7.1 One tool to rule them all

In the next chapter I'll show you examples of *Dockerfile* files for several development technologies. What I'd like you to note beforehand is that the processes we use don't depend on the development technology. Whether Java, Python, .NET Core, Node.JS, PHP (or many other ones), the same instructions are used to build, ship and deploy the applications.

This is a major benefit in many environments. If you're part of a team, chances are that many technologies are being used; however, the way to build, ship and deploy the applications depends on the applications' development tools. Having a single tool to manage them all yields several benefits:

- members of the team that use one development stack can help those using others;
- a single CI/CD process and common tools can be used across most projects, and improvements benefit to all of those projects;

Practically, whatever the technology the same instructions are used to build, ship and deploy the applications.

Something around those lines:

Build, deliver on the CI/CD server

```
docker build -t learnbook/my-server .
docker push learnbook/my-server
```

Deploy on the target machine

```
docker run --rm -it -p 80:80 learnbook/my-server
```

7.2 Building rationally: easy CI

Note that I wrote *"build"* in the preceding chapter, while most of what we did in our *Dockerfile* files was pack our software, not build it.

But I really meant *build*. Docker is not only a technology to pack your software, but it can actually build it. When you build an image, you are actually running software inside a container (the *RUN* commands in the *Dockerfile* file). Since those *RUN* commands run in an image, the image describes the dependencies needed to build the software.

Remember those hard times you had as a developer? You cloned some code only to realize that building it took you a day since you needed to install many build dependencies and SDK tools. Once you decide to build your software inside images, all you need is Docker.

Whether on a development machine or CI/CD server: Docker. This is a major benefit for the projects I've been working on and I have no doubt that you're going to benefit from it.

In fact, that can even be taken a step further: you can use the same Docker machines to build and run your software. Instead of having a build server and test server, you can actually use the test server to build. Going a step further with orchestration, you can use the same Kubernetes cluster to host your deployments *and* build your code - but that's another story.

Let's take an ASP.NET Core application as an example. ASP.NET Core requires us to restore the NuGet packages referenced by the *.csproj* files, then build the source code (C# files) into DLLs and pack in any necessary dependencies. This may be done with the following *Dockerfile* definition:

Dockerfile

```
FROM microsoft/dotnet:2.2-sdk AS builder
WORKDIR /app

COPY . .
RUN dotnet restore
RUN dotnet publish --output /out/ --configuration Relea\
se

EXPOSE 80
ENTRYPOINT ["dotnet", "aspnet-core.dll"]
```

The *FROM* instruction makes sure we have the tools needed to build (SDK) then calls the *dotnet restore* and *dotnetpublish* to get our code ready for deployment inside the image. This allows us to run *docker build* on the CI server or a developer machine and get an image that contains built files. When the container starts on a server *(docker run)*, the *ENTRYPOINT* instruction simply makes sure that our code is started inside the container.

Since the *Dockerfile* definition is archived with our source code, we are sure that we'll keep the build instructions synchronized with our code, and different branches may even have different *Dockerfile* definitions.

There's a problem with the resulting image however. Can you guess it?

7.3 Multi-stage dockerfiles

The problem with the image we created above is that it's fat. It weights **1730 MB**! This is because it contains the build tools: tools like *dotnet restore* and *dotnet publish*. We do not need those tools. Also, it contains the source code and intermediate build artifacts.

We could use the *RUN* command to try and clean the image: delete intermediate build artifacts, uninstall build tools, delete source code, but that would be tedious. Time to remember that containers are like cheap, disposable machines. Let's dispose of the build machine and grab a brand new one that has only the runtime installed!

Docker has a neat way to do this: use a single *Dockerfile* file with distinct sections. An image can be named simply by adding *AS <name>* at the end of the *FROM* instruction. Consider the following simplified *Dockerfile* file:

```
FROM fat-image AS builder
...

FROM small-image
COPY --from=builder /result .
...
```

It defines two images, but only the last one will be kept as the result of the *docker build* command. The filesystem that has been created in the first image, named *builder*, is made available to the second image thanks to the *--from* argument of the *COPY* command. It states that the */result* folder from the *builder* image will be copied to the current working directory of the second image.

This technique allows you to benefit from the tools available in *fat-image* but get a resulting image with only the environment defined in the *small-image* it's based on. And you can have many stages in a *Dockerfile* file when necessary.

Here is an actual example. I just improved the *Dockerfile* file shown in the preceding chapter, so that this time it uses a multi-stage build:

Dockerfile

```
FROM microsoft/dotnet:2.2-sdk AS builder
WORKDIR /app

COPY *.csproj .
RUN dotnet restore

COPY . .
RUN dotnet publish --output /out/ --configuration Relea\
se

FROM microsoft/dotnet:2.2-aspnetcore-runtime-alpine
WORKDIR /app
COPY --from=builder /out .
EXPOSE 80
ENTRYPOINT ["dotnet", "aspnet-core.dll"]
```

In the first part, I use the full and fat image that contains the whole SDK in order to build my application to an /out directory. Then this image is trashed, except that the contents of its /out directory are copied to the /app directory of a second image. The second image is based on a runtime image, much smaller than the SDK image. In order to make it even lighter, I used an alpine-based image.

When I build an image from that multi-stage definition I get an image that weights only **161 MB**. That's a 91% improvement over the image size!

You definitely want to produce small images for the reasons we saw in the Size matters section, so if you plan to generate artifacts inside Docker, make sure to use multi-stage *Dockerfile* files.

8. Docker with common development profiles

We saw how an application can be packaged into a Dockerfile, and you should be good to go. However, when creating your first images you may hesitate over some common patterns. I'd rather you didn't loose time with that, so I listed in this chapter some basic application images for common development technologies. Just pick your own.

Each subchapter is divided into two parts:

- *Result* points you to the resulting image (I published them on the Docker Hub so you can run them right away);
- *Files* details the files (especially the *Dockerfile* file) that I used to create the image.

8.1 .NET Core

Result

The resulting image is published as *learnbook/aspnet-core-server*. You can run a container from it with the following command:

106 Docker with common development profiles

```
docker run --rm -it -p 8088:80 learnbook/aspnetcore-ser\
ver
```

Then point your browser to http://localhost:8088

Files

> You may find those files in the the *code/common-development-profiles/demos/aspnet-core* folder.

A static HTML file to be served:

wwwroot/index.htm
```
<h1>Hello !</h1>
<p>This page is served by ASP.NET Core</p>
<p>Try our <a href="/v1/square/4">multiply API</a>.</p>
```

A REST API coded with ASP.NET Core MVC:

ApiController.cs

```csharp
using System;
using Microsoft.AspNetCore.Mvc;

namespace aspnet_core
{
    [Route("v1")]
    [ApiController]
    public class ValuesController : ControllerBase
    {
        // GET api/values
        [HttpGet("square/{value}")]
        public IActionResult Square(double value)
        {
            var result = Math.Pow(value, 2);
            return Ok(new {
                value = value,
                result = result
            });
        }
    }
}
```

Configuration of the HTTP server (middleware and dependency injection):

Startup.cs

```csharp
using Microsoft.AspNetCore.Builder;
using Microsoft.AspNetCore.Hosting;
using Microsoft.AspNetCore.Mvc;
using Microsoft.Extensions.Configuration;
using Microsoft.Extensions.DependencyInjection;

namespace aspnet_core
{
    public class Startup
    {
        public void ConfigureServices(
            IServiceCollection services)
        {
            services.AddMvc().SetCompatibilityVersion(
                CompatibilityVersion.Version_2_1);
        }

        public void Configure(
            IApplicationBuilder app,
            IHostingEnvironment env
        )
        {
            app.UseDeveloperExceptionPage();
            app.UseDefaultFiles();
            app.UseStaticFiles();
            app.UseMvc();
        }
    }
}
```

Spin up the HTTP server:

Program.cs

```
using Microsoft.AspNetCore;
using Microsoft.AspNetCore.Hosting;

namespace aspnet_core
{
    public class Program
    {
        public static void Main(string[] args)
        {
            WebHost.CreateDefaultBuilder(args)
                .UseStartup<Startup>()
                .Build()
                .Run();
        }
    }
}
```

The .csproj file containing build instructions:

Docker with common development profiles

aspnet-core.csproj

```xml
<Project Sdk="Microsoft.NET.Sdk.Web">

  <PropertyGroup>
    <TargetFramework>netcoreapp2.2</TargetFramework>
  </PropertyGroup>

  <ItemGroup>
    <Folder Include="wwwroot\" />
  </ItemGroup>

  <ItemGroup>
    <PackageReference
      Include="Microsoft.AspNetCore.App" />
    <PackageReference
      Include="Microsoft.AspNetCore.Razor.Design"
      Version="2.2"
      PrivateAssets="All" />
  </ItemGroup>

</Project>
```

Definition of the image to build:

Dockerfile

```
# Use an image with the SDK for compilation
FROM microsoft/dotnet:2.2-sdk AS builder
WORKDIR /app

# Get the build file
COPY *.csproj .
# Optinal. Run this first so that it is cached
RUN dotnet restore

# Get the source code inside the image
COPY . .
RUN dotnet publish --output /out/ --configuration Relea\
se

# Create a lightweight image
FROM microsoft/dotnet:2.2-aspnetcore-runtime-alpine
WORKDIR /app
# Copy compiled artifacts from previous image
COPY --from=builder /out .
EXPOSE 80
ENTRYPOINT ["dotnet", "aspnet-core.dll"]
```

8.2 Java

Result

The resulting image is published as *learnbook/java*. You can run a container from it with the following command:

```
docker run --rm learnbook/java
```

Files

> You may find those files in the the *code/common-development-profiles/demos/java* folder.

Simple Java source code:

Hello.java
```java
class Hello{
  public static void main(String[] args) {
    System.out.println("Java in a container.");
  }
}
```

Docker image definition:

Dockerfile

```
# Use an image with the SDK for compilation
FROM openjdk:8-jdk-alpine AS builder
WORKDIR /out
# Get the source code inside the image
COPY *.java .
# Compile source code
RUN javac Hello.java

# Create a lightweight image
FROM openjdk:8-jre-alpine
# Copy compiled artifacts from previous image
COPY --from=builder /out/*.class .
CMD ["java", "Hello"]
```

8.3 Node.JS

Result

The resulting image is published as *learnbook/node-server*. You can run a container from it with the following command:

```
docker run --rm -it -p 8087:80 learnbook/node-server
```

Then point your browser to http://localhost:8087

Files

> You may find those files in the the *code/common-development-profiles/demos/nodejs* folder.

A static HTML file to be served:

www/index.htm
```
<h1>Hello !</h1>
<p>This page is served by Node.JS</p>
<p>Try our <a href="/v1/square/4">multiply API</a>.</p>
```

Define and run an HTTP server, a static files server and a REST API:

index.js
```
const HTTP_PORT = 80;

const cors = require('cors');
const express = require('express');
const path = require('path');

var sourcesDirectory = path.resolve(__dirname, 'www');
var app = express();
app.use(cors());

// API
app.get('/v1/square/:value', function (req, res) {
```

```
    const value = req.params.value;
    const square = Math.pow(value, 2);
    res.send({
        value,
        square
    });
});

// Static files
app.use(express.static(sourcesDirectory, {
    index: 'index.htm',
    extensions: ['htm']
}));

var server = require('http').createServer(app);
server.listen(HTTP_PORT);

console.log(`Listening on http://localhost:${HTTP_PORT}\
`);
```

List dependencies that will need to be restored during the build:

116 Docker with common development profiles

package.json

```
{
  "name": "node-server",
  "version": "1.0.0",
  "main": "index.js",
  "scripts": {
    "start": "node index.js"
  },
  "dependencies": {
    "async": "^2.4.1",
    "cors": "^2.8.3",
    "express": "^4.15.2"
  }
}
```

Docker image definition:

Dockerfile

```
FROM node:10-alpine

# Create app directory
RUN mkdir -p /usr/src/app
WORKDIR /usr/src/app

# Install app dependencies
COPY package.json /usr/src/app/
RUN npm install

WORKDIR /usr/src/app
```

```
# Bundle app source
COPY . /usr/src/app/

EXPOSE 80

CMD ["npm", "start"]
```

8.4 PHP

Result

The resulting image is published as *learnbook/php-server*. You can run a container from it with the following command:

```
docker run --rm -it -p 8090:80 learnbook/php-server
```

Then point your browser to http://localhost:8090

Files

> You may find those files in the the *code/common-development-profiles/demos/php* folder.

A static HTML file to be served:

118 Docker with common development profiles

index.php

```
<h1>Hello !</h1>
<p>This page is served by PHP</p>
<p>Try our <a href="/v1/square/4">multiply API</a>.</p>
```

A simple REST API definition:

myapi.php

```
<?php

    $url = $_REQUEST['rquest'];
    $components = explode("/", $url);
    $value = (float)$components[2];
    $square = $value * $value;
    header("Content-Type: application/json; charset=UTF-8\
");
    $result = (object) array(
        'value' => $value,
        'square' => $square
    );
    echo json_encode($result);

?>
```

URL rewriting rules for Apache:

.htaccess

```
<IfModule mod_rewrite.c>
    RewriteEngine On

    RewriteCond %{REQUEST_FILENAME} -f [OR]
    RewriteCond %{REQUEST_FILENAME} -d
    RewriteRule ^(.+) - [PT,L]

    RewriteRule ^(v1/.*)$ myapi.php?rquest=$1 [L]

</IfModule>
```

Docker image definition:

Dockerfile

```
FROM php:7.0-apache

# Install Apache module
RUN a2enmod rewrite

COPY . /var/www/html/
```

8.5 Python

Result

The resulting image is published as *learnbook/python-server*. You can run a container from it with the following command:

```
docker run --rm -it -p 8089:5000 learnbook/python-server
```

Then point your browser to http://localhost:8089

Files

> You may find those files in the the *code/common-development-profiles/demos/python* folder.

A static HTML file to be served:

templates/index.htm
```
<h1>Hello !</h1>
<p>This page is served by Python</p>
<p>Try our <a href="/v1/square/4">multiply API</a>.</p>
```

Define and run an HTTP server, a static files server and a REST API:

server.py

```python
from flask import Flask
from flask import render_template
from flask import request, jsonify

app = Flask(__name__)

@app.route('/v1/square/<int:value>')
def show_user_profile(value):
    square = value * value
    return jsonify(value=value, square=square)

@app.route('/')
def hello():
    return render_template('index.htm')
```

Docker image definition:

Dockerfile

```
FROM python:3.7-stretch

# Install modules
RUN pip install Flask

# Needed by the Flask module
ENV FLASK_APP=server.py

# Copy source files into the image
COPY templates ./templates
COPY server.py .
```

```
EXPOSE 5000

CMD ["flask", "run", "--host=0.0.0.0"]
```

I need you, super-hero !

Thank you so much for reading this book. I do hope that it helps you understand and get confident with Docker.

As a reader, you are kind of a super-hero: you gain the power to package and deploy your applications seamlessly and make computers more useful.

Guess what? You have another superpower: to rate this book on the site where you purchased it. You may feel it's nothing, but it is super important for auto-edited books like this one. Please, take some minutes of your precious time to rate this book. That counts a lot for independent authors like myself!

9. More about Running containers

At this point, you should be good to go with Docker. Here are a few more tips that should make your life with Docker smoother.

9.1 Restart mode

When creating a container, you have the choice to set a restart mode. It tells Docker what to do when a container stops. A restart mode is set with the `--restart` switch.

When running server containers like we did earlier, we want them to always be up, so it is very tempting to use the *always* restart mode. For instance:

```
docker run -d -p 80 --restart always nginx
```

It works great. Should the container start or the Docker host itself restart, the container will restart so that it has a high uptime. But it actually works too well: if you try to stop the container using the *docker stop* command, it will not stop.

That's probably not what you want. If you want your container to be always running *except* when you explicitly stop it, use the *unless_stopped* restart mode:

```
docker run -d -p 80 --restart unless-stopped nginx
```

That way your container will almost always be up, except when you don't want it to.

9.2 Monitoring

High availability Docker servers are monitored with tools that are up to the task, such as, collecting your logs and usage statistics. For simple needs or your development box however, you may simply use the following command:

```
docker stats
```

This will output a live list of running containers plus information about how much resources they consume on the host machine. Like a *docker ps* extended with live resource usage data.

Here's an example output:

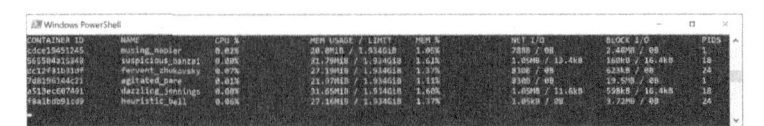

Sorry that was small. Here's the most interesting part zoomed in:

CPU %	MEM USAGE / LIMIT	MEM %
0.02%	20.8MiB / 1.934GiB	1.05%
0.00%	31.79MiB / 1.934GiB	1.61%
0.07%	27.19MiB / 1.934GiB	1.37%
0.01%	21.97MiB / 1.934GiB	1.11%
0.00%	31.65MiB / 1.934GiB	1.60%
0.06%	27.16MiB / 1.934GiB	1.37%

9.3 Reclaim your disk

Creating images and running containers, consumes disk space that later on you want to reclaim. Here are some ways disk space is consumed unknowingly:

- stopped containers that were not removed (using the --rm switch on the *docker run* command or using the *docker rm* command once they are stopped);
- unused images: images that are not referenced by other images or containers;
- dangling images: images that have no name (this happens when you *docker build* an image with the same tag as before, the new one replaces it and the old one becomes dangling);
- unused volumes.

Manually removing these one by can be tedious, but there are garbage collection commands that can help with that.

Most commands ask for an interactive confirmation, but if you want to run them unattended you can add the -f switch.

Here are the commands you can run to remove the items that you don't need:

```
docker container prune -f
docker volume prune -f
docker image prune -f
```

Note that only dangling images are removed. Unused images are kept, which is fine if a network connection is scarce or unavailable because it means you keep base images that *may* be useful later on. In case you want to remove all unused images, just use the following command:

```
docker image prune --all
```

9.4 Orchestration basics

In this chapter we saw some tools (the `--restart-mode` switch, the *docker stats* command) that help keep your containers running and keep an eye on them. This is good for starters. However, if you highly rely on containers and/or have high workloads, using such tools and automating their use will become tedious.

Imagine coding calls to create or update containers, and to remove them when necessary. How will you update your containers when you publish new versions? Since running containers is cheap, you may want to perform rolling updates so that your application isn't down during updates. In a rolling update, a new container is started with the newest image, and once it is ready users are routed to it, then the old container is removed. Imagine coding that: it's going to be tedious.

Now factor in the possibility that several Docker hosts may need to run your containers (either for large workloads, scaling out or simply good reliability). In such cases you will need to setup a reverse proxy and have it route users to the appropriate containers. You really don't want to maintain script files that do this.

Good news: you don't need to worry about that. Those problems are solved by orchestration tools. When such needs arise, it will be time to use an orchestration tool like Docker Swarm or Kubernetes.

Kubernetes or Docker Swarm receive your orders and apply them. You create a cluster of servers (a single server is fine also), then you feed your Kubernetes or Docker Swarm with a file that states which containers you want, how to expose them to the outside world, and how many containers should be ran for each image. Your orchestrator will make sure that happens.

Here is an example Kubernetes file:

```
apiVersion: apps/v1beta1
kind: Deployment
spec:
  replicas: 2
  template:
    metadata:
      labels:
        app: core-server
    spec:
      containers:
      - image: learnbook/aspnetcore-server:1.1
        ports:
        - containerPort: 80
        env:
        - name: ASPNETCORE_ENVIRONMENT
          value: "Release"
---
apiVersion: v1
kind: Service
spec:
  type: LoadBalancer
  ports:
  - port: 80
  selector:
    app: core-server
```

In spite of the apparent complexity, it's not that hard. Sending it to the cluster (using the *kubectl* command) makes sure that I get my application running as two containers exposed over the internet with a load balancer. Nice, isn't it?

Better yet: need to upgrade or run more or less containers? Update the file stating your new needs, feed it to the orchestrator and it will take care of things like rolling upgrades. Look at my modified file:

```
apiVersion: apps/v1beta1
kind: Deployment
spec:
  replicas: 10
  template:
    metadata:
      labels:
        app: core-server
    spec:
      containers:
      - image: learnbook/aspnetcore-server:1.2
        ports:
        - containerPort: 80
        env:
        - name: ASPNETCORE_ENVIRONMENT
          value: "Release"
---
apiVersion: v1
kind: Service
spec:
  type: LoadBalancer
  ports:
  - port: 80
  selector:
    app: core-server
```

I only changed the *replicas* and *image* values in order to ask for 10 containers and have them run a more recent 1.2 image. I simply send it to the cluster (again using the *kubectl* command), and Kubernetes proceeds with the operations necessary to reach that state taking into account the existing state. It will:

1. start 10 containers running the 1.2 image;
2. wait for 2 containers to be ready;
3. route the users to the 2 containers that are ready;
4. stop and remove the previous two containers that run the 1.1 image;
5. as the 8 more containers become available, route users to them;
6. load balance the incoming traffic to the 10 containers.

Probably something you wouldn't dream of if you were managing actual servers, even if they were virtualized. You took a huge step forward moving your application into containers, and moving those containers to an orchestrator is another giant step forward.

Orchestration is out of the scope for this book so I won't continue here. But guess what? It will be the subject for my next book: *Learn Kubernetes*.

Image attributions

- Classic ship loading: public domain, from Wikimedia Commons[1]
- Container ship loading: public domain, Tvabutzku1234, from Wikimedia Commons[2].
- Freight train: public domain, G-Man March 2005, from Wikimedia Commons[3], originally uploaded to the English Wikipedia.

---

[1] https://commons.wikimedia.org/wiki/File:Korean-war-merchant-marine-load.jpg#file
[2] https://commons.wikimedia.org/wiki/File:Container_ship_Yorktown_Express_(2).jpg
[3] https://commons.wikimedia.org/wiki/File:WCML_freight_train.jpg

A word from the author

I sincerely hope you enjoyed reading this book as much as I liked writing it and that you quickly become proficient enough with containerizing your applications and Docker.

If you would like to get in touch you can use :

- email: books@aweil.fr
- Facebook: https://facebook.com/learncollection

In case your project needs it, I'm also available for speaking, teaching, consulting and coding, all around the world.

If you liked this book, you probably saved a lot of time thanks to it. I'd be very grateful if you took some minutes of your precious time to leave a comment on the site where you purchased this book. Thanks a ton!

The Learn collection

This book is part of the *Learn collection*.

The *Learn collection* allows developers to self-teach new technologies in a matter of days.

Published books

- Learn ASP.NET Core MVC[4]
- Learn ASP.NET MVC[5]
- Learn Docker[6]
- Learn Meteor[7]
- Learn Microservices[8]
- Learn WPF MVVM[9]

To be published

- Learn Kubernetes
- Learn Unit Testing

---

[4] https://leanpub.com/netcore
[5] https://leanpub.com/aspnetmvc
[6] https://leanpub.com/dock
[7] https://leanpub.com/learnmeteor
[8] https://leanpub.com/micro
[9] https://leanpub.com/learnwpf

Printed in Great Britain
by Amazon